Essentials for Fundraising and Development

MISSIO NEXUS IMPROVE SERIES

Essentials for Fundraising and Development

A Collection of Best Practices, Ideas, and Strategies

Michael R. VanHuis and Heather Pubols, eds.

Missio Nexus, Wheaton, IL
Published 2020
Printed in the United States of America

ISBN-13: 979-8-597-57874-3 (paper)

Scripture quotations marked (ESV) are from The ESV® Bible (The Holy
Bible, English Standard Version®), copyright © 2001 by Crossway, a
publishing ministry of Good News Publishers. Used by permission. All
rights reserved.

Scripture quotations marked (KJV) are taken from The Authorized (King
James) Version. Public domain.

Scripture quotations marked (NIV) are taken from the Holy Bible, New
International Version®, NIV®. Copyright © 1973, 1978, 1984, 2011 by
Biblica, Inc.™ Used by permission of Zondervan. All rights reserved
worldwide. www.zondervan.comThe "NIV" and "New International
Version" are trademarks registered in the United States Patent and
Trademark Office by Biblica, Inc.™

Scripture quotations marked (NLT) are taken from the Holy Bible, New
Living Translation, copyright ©1996, 2004, 2015 by Tyndale House
Foundation. Used by permission of Tyndale House Publishers, a Division
of Tyndale House Ministries, Carol Stream, Illinois 60188. All rights
reserved.

Chapter eleven was originally published in a slightly different form in
The Journey into DoingGoodBetter, Steve Kaloper (2015), chapter seven.
Reprinted by permission of the author.

Our thanks to Emily Amundson for proofreading.

The cover was designed and interior typeset by Kurtis Amundson.

Contents

Preface

It was a cold and blustery fall day. I landed at the Hartford, Connecticut airport with a list of potential donors to visit in the area. As I left the airport and started driving toward my hotel, two of my contacts canceled their meetings. Over the next few hours, I reached out to two other contacts who did not return my calls. I ended up with one meeting for lunch the following day.

The next day I arrived early at a classic northeastern diner to meet with a couple that had given to projects in the past with our mission agency. A few minutes later an older lady arrived alone, and we worked through those uncomfortable moments of realizing we were the ones meeting with each other. Her husband had decided he did not want to come. I barely introduced myself when she let me know they would not be giving to any more of our organization's projects. I didn't even get a chance to update her on past projects, let alone dive into a presentation.

I put my notes away, ordered coffee, and realized that this would not be about promoting our new initiative. This visit was all about hearing, listening, and being the minister on duty to this woman. I left the meeting only to find out that a storm was approaching, and all flights were being scrubbed. I rushed to the airport to find my flight canceled. I had one chance to grab a taxi with two strangers and head to a neighboring airport to get the last flight that would not take me back to Chicago but to Charlotte and then to Chicago.

My three-hour flight turned into eight hours of travel. Tired and confused, I sat on the plane flying from Charlotte to Chicago, when I should have already been home, wondering what the point was. A small quiet voice reminded me that God is sovereign. Yes but ... time, money, and effort for what? That voice said, "A woman needed a minister, and I put you there for that reason." I still had much to learn about being a major gifts officer, but that day I realized an important lesson: relationship trumps transaction.

MISSIO NEXUS SEEKS TO CATALYZE RELATIONSHIPS, collaboration and ideas within the Great Commission community. For over one hundred years this association has strengthened mission agencies by providing opportunities for mission focused people to learn, meet and engage together around critical issues and priorities for global evangelism and church planting.

As we continue to engage with leaders of mission agencies, one of the greatest needs is training and tools in the arena for fundraising and development. With the help of a partner foundation, we are endeavoring to not only provide new training tools, but to begin thinking through the present and future realties of funding Great Commission work.

It has been said that the right activities lead to the right outcomes. I fully believe this. But that begs the question, what are the right activities? In this book we will help you discover a few of the right fundraising and development activities.

Key fundraising practitioners collaborated with us to bring practical insights for you and your agencies to help you determine how to get your ministry funded and flourishing.

The original intended audience for this book were small to mid-sized ministries that did not have a plan for fundraising or had only established small gains in this area. But it has become clear as the chapters have been submitted that no matter where you are in your knowledge and execution of fundraising activities, this book and its content will be of great benefit.

James 5:16 says, "The effectual fervent prayers of a righteous man availeth much" (KJV). As you enter the world of fundraising, it becomes quickly apparent that being a hard worker is not enough. Instead, this is a spiritual act of faith and dependence upon God. Only through prayer and seeking God to move in the hearts and minds of his people will you see the resources provided for his work among the nations. You can labor all day with good work, but unless it is consecrated in prayer it will availeth little and leave you frustrated and worn out.

Prayer begins with our boards and senior leaders as they ensure funds are raised for the activities that God established and not just things that feed your ego or make our organizations look good. Prayer guides your teams and staff as you consider the culture of your organization and the way in which you will approach potential resource partners. Prayer comes before every phone call, email, text message, and meeting. It precedes every conversation and follows every interaction.

Prayer increases our awareness of our dependence upon God and not on our own efforts. Without prayer our efforts become hollow and self-serving and, in the end, unproductive. With prayer, we are transformed into people dependent on a sovereign God who will direct his resources to meet the needs of his work among the nations.

AS YOU BEGIN THIS BOOK, I would encourage you, even now, to spend a few moments in prayer. I hope and pray that God has something new and fresh for you as you read the ideas and concepts that have been curated in the following pages. You will identify several recurring themes as you engage in the following chapters.

CHARACTER MATTERS: Knowledge without character leads to short cuts and tactics that leave potential partners feeling used. Strong character fosters healthy relationships that enables your ministry to flourish and partners to celebrate the opportunity to steward resources effectively. Character is essential in approaching potential partners, reporting information to foundations and in the people you hire to be part of your development team.

INTENTIONALITY MATTERS: Take time to know your culture and know your comfort level with different fundraising strategies. Be intentional with knowing your audience whether that is a couple you are meeting for a first time or a foundation that you are preparing a grant request. Intentionality takes time, but the benefits are exponential. Intentionality values relationships over transactions.

INTEGRATION MATTERS: Placing all the weight of fundraising on one person may produce short-term results, but long-term it leads to frustration and burnout. Fundraising is a team sport. Integration of efforts from the board to individual missionaries is essential. It results in a collective effort that leads to broader impact and sustainability for the organization and those directly caring out development efforts.

RELATIONSHIP MATTERS: As you engage with potential donors, your mindset needs to be one of relationship building and stewarding. Too often donors feel like they are simply receiving a sales pitch. Your mindset in engagement should deeply value establishing relationships and caring for people. It is an honor to help people see the broader picture of global needs and how God has equipped them to serve through giving. Relationship is what you want to achieve, not securing a transaction.

DISCIPLESHIP MATTERS: Relationships with potential and current donors go beyond interpersonal. The heart of fundraising is discipleship. It is an invitation you give to another to journey more deeply into God's mission. As you walk with donors, God works to bring transformation not only in the lives of those your ministry serves, but also in your donors' hearts as well as yours.

ATTUNEMENT WITH GOD MATTERS: When your plans and efforts inevitably fail along the way, as happened to me in Hartford, remember that you are nested in a bigger story – God's story. As kingdom workers, sometimes the King's plans diverge from ours. Don't miss the moments God gives you to attune to what he is doing as well as the opportunities he presents to discover ways to work more effectively.

Each chapter will provide you with questions to ponder and resources to allow you to take next steps. Heather Pubols and I, along with the writers of these chapters, hope that you will take time to deeply reflect and consider the ideas and suggestions you will find in the following pages. You are not alone. All of us are learning and growing together. We are each deeply dependent on our Heavenly Father to steward donors and resources for his glory and his name to be proclaimed among the nations.

MICHAEL R. VANHUIS
Vice President
Missio Nexus

CHAPTER 1

Creating a Culture of Philanthropy

By Barbara Bowman

ONE DAY AS I WAS WALKING down the hallway, I ran into our CFO as he rushed to a meeting about an upcoming fundraising event. This annual event brought together donors, leaders, fundraising staff, board members and mission partners. I noticed a small label with the letters *IAATF* in large letters taped to his nametag. I stopped, stared, and threw up my hands in defeat.

"What does IAATF mean?" I asked.

He responded, "It's all about the field." The *field* was our overseas program locations where our missionaries served, and our mission was carried out. He continued, "The purpose of everything we do here at headquarters is to enable and ensure people living in the remote corners of the world experience the love of Jesus."

As I continued walking, I kept thinking about what the CFO said. I agreed that our organization, like all missions, existed to share the gospel, but tension still rose inside me. Then it hit me. Our organization served more than just the *field* overseas. The fundraising team saw *donors* as their front-line ministry, and as the chief advancement officer, I saw my *direct reports* as people I led and discipled. In fact, the work of missionaries abroad and fundraisers working from a home office are not all that different.

Development leaders and fundraisers are also called to discipleship.

Development leaders and fundraisers are also called to discipleship and ministry so that missionaries in other places can fulfill their purpose on that front-line.

I continued to unpack this discomfort over the next week as I recalled various other disturbing statements and observations. Someone once joked that my department was a "piggy bank." I noted that not every board member contributed financially. Leaders regularly questioned expenses for development activities and staff, and they did not prioritize investments in donor relationships and field experiences.

A troubling reality emerged. The organizational culture did not support our fundraising work. Like many mission organizations, fundraising started with a deputized fundraising approach: missionary staff each raised funds for salaries and ministry expenses while the headquarters staff operated on a fixed percentage of those raised funds. This long-standing tradition was deeply entrenched in the culture. Eventually, it became necessary to grow our fundraising capacity, but the culture never shifted. It needed to adapt so that both fundraising models would be accepted and resourced. A culture of philanthropy for the cause of the organization needed to be embraced alongside the long-held culture of supporting individual missionaries.

What is Organizational Culture?

I define organizational culture as the collective attitude that characterizes and impacts the ways an organization's people perceive one another and work together. Culture is crafted on both conscious and subconscious levels. The older an organization is the more likely each generation has left its mark. Culture creation may be one of the most significant and lasting legacies for an executive team and board. Many global mission organizations are seventy to one hundred years old, and organizational culture is deeply entrenched and complex to deconstruct or change.

My observation is that most global mission organizations view fundraising as an important function for a group of staff at their main office in North America, rather than an organizational-wide ministry of philanthropy. Changing this reality is well worth the effort on many levels. Most importantly, it will increase charitable income for both the organization and individual missionary support.

Culture does not change overnight, but with a concerted effort, starting with the board and executive leadership, change will happen. The key is it needs to be nurtured and cared for like new grass seed that eventually roots and flourishes into a strong drought-resistant lawn. If you lead development or advancement for your organization, always keep culture change at the top of your strategic plans, not just one time.

There are several reasons why culture has become an important topic in the last ten years. The top reason is fierce competition for philanthropic dollars. Organizations that rely on the collaboration and cooperation of all board, leaders, and staff in sourcing charitable dollars for their important mission receive the best results. When one hundred staff reach out to their networks on social media platforms, mention the impact of their organization and contribute their own ideas internally so more people hear *the story*, the number of people seeing and engaging with your cause is multiplied exponentially. This is far more effective then relying on ten people in the fundraising department to do the same.

Another reality is that donors do not enjoy being a piggy bank. Donors want a relationship instead of a financial transaction. Increasingly, donors want to give strategically, build new momentum for ministry in the field, and have a partnership where their voice matters and their sweat equity is leveraged. Lastly, stakeholder communications are changing rapidly with technological advances and social media platforms. More content and stories are needed to fill the space across channels from blogs, podcasts, media clips, Facebook campaigns, Instagram, and others. Specialized communication strategies are in demand for major, mid-level, and mass-level donor segmentations.

Robert Gass founder of the Transformation Project says, "Fundraising is limited more by organizational culture and structure than by lack of strategic or tactical know-how." Changing culture is more than an intellectual exercise. Gass goes on to say that sustainable organizational change only comes about when employees are willing to engage in three places: *hearts and minds* – feelings and thoughts; *behavior* – choices and norms; and *structures* – the external processes and practices that organize activities. If there is only an emphasis on external processes and practices without a change of heart or belief system, the change is likely to be short lived.

According to the report *Beyond Fundraising: What Does it Mean to Create a Culture of Philanthropy* there are four core areas that lay the foundation for a culture of accountability:

FUNDRAISING IS A SHARED RESPONSIBILITY. Raising funds is not only one person's job or the job of one department or board committee but universally shared and valued by everyone – paid staff, deputized missionaries, volunteers, the CEO, board and constituents. This does not mean that everyone dedicates one hundred percent of their work efforts to it, but everyone shares in some level of fundraising effort, collaboration, and success.

FUNDRAISING IS INTEGRATED AND ALIGNED WITH THE MISSION. Fund development is a valued and mission-aligned component of the organization's overall work, rather than a standalone function or of a lesser strategic importance. Building a culture of philanthropy means viewing fundraising as a tactic for achieving larger

The best place to begin a culture change is with an honest assessment of your current culture.

programmatic goals and mission, rather than an end unto itself or paying for overhead.

FUNDRAISING FOCUSES ON ENGAGEMENT. Fund development is no longer separated from cross-channel engagement. People connect with nonprofits through multiple channels (e.g., social media, volunteering, blogs, meet ups, petitions) and engage with them in multiple ways (e.g., as donors, volunteers, board members, constituents). Donors own how they engage and are not passive in the process.

FUNDRAISING EMPHASIZES STRONG DONOR RELATIONS. Donors are authentic partners in the work, sometimes known as *builders*, not simply as dollar signs, or *buyers*. These organizations establish systems to build strong relationships and support donors' connection to the work. Donors receive credible ways of giving that connect with their unique hearts and passions.

Rating Your Culture

The best place to begin a culture change is with an honest assessment of your current culture. Then you can identify what key areas need to be addressed to move incrementally towards a development friendly culture. Approach the process without judgment or blame. Use a sliding scale to rate several factors which are demonstrated in organizations with thriving philanthropy cultures using the following questions.

Does your mission statement encompass donors as vital to the work being carried out overseas? Do you work as hard to see transformation in your donors as you do with your beneficiaries?

NO ————————————————————— YES

Does your organization respond to one of the world's greatest needs and your donors' passions? Do these change in unison and is open dialogue a norm? Does one inform the other and vice versa?

NO ————————————————————— YES

Are requests for funding based on the mutual desires of donors and the organization to fulfill the mission rather than by only internal needs? Do you ask, "What would our donors think about this new idea or new initiative?"

NO ————————————————————— YES

Do all staff and board members know how to communicate the organization's *story* of impact and the way donor gifts make a direct difference?

NO ————————————————————— YES

Do all staff know the strategic funding priorities in every budget cycle? Can they speak about them with anyone in their own network they encounter casually or formally?

NO ————————————————————— YES

How is communication with donors handled? Is it focused on donors making a difference, creating impact, and stewarding God's resources or does it instead use *shortfall* language and request help so *we* can make a difference?

Do the board, leadership, and the entire staff embrace fundraising as a noble ministry that is essential to carry out the organization's mission?

When a donor walks through the front doors of your organization, do all staff treat them as equals and honored guests? Do donors have direct access and relationships with staff from your field operations team, human resources, finance, and other key areas beyond the fundraising team? Would a donor feel comfortable arranging a visit to a field program and would the field team be willing to host them with little to no hesitation?

Does the CEO and the entire executive team share the annual fundraising goals and successes? Do they solve fundraising problems that emerge throughout the year together?

Do field leaders have close and trusted relationships with fundraising colleagues? Do they spend time in each other's contexts and support each other's needs? Are requests from the fundraising team considered essential and not an interruption to field programs?

Has the marketing team experienced the impact of the *story* first-hand on the field? Do they receive impact stories on a regular basis because they are in long-term relationships with field staff?

NO ——————————————————————————— YES

Are board members as excited about the fundraising report on the agenda as they are about field program reports? Do board members personally know any of the staff from your fundraising and marketing departments?

NO ——————————————————————————— YES

Do board members open their networks gladly? Do they regularly speak about your organization in their own social networks in addition to hosting and attending donor events, vision trips, and weekend gatherings?

NO ——————————————————————————— YES

At the end of a successful fundraising campaign, do all organizational staff celebrate the outcomes or does only the fundraising team?

NO ——————————————————————————— YES

Do publications feature a donor story, describe impact, and tell how to give? Or do publications only inform or feature field stories?

NO ——————————————————————————— YES

Does your CEO embrace fundraising and feel comfortable sharing impact stories and strategic organizational goals? Does he or she spend significant time (30%–50%) meeting with donors and seeking their input? Does the CEO know many donors beyond their portfolio by name? Do fundraising leaders feel like the CEO is a part of their team?

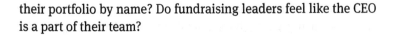

Are your fundraising and marketing departments viewed as an income centers rather than only expenses? Are their expenses seen within the context of the income they generate?

Does your fundraising team leader serve on the executive team and report directly to the CEO? Can he or she access the board and speak regularly to them?

Does your organization's strategic plan address costs for growing impact or field programs and resources needed to raise the charitable income? Is the conversation a multi-directional one involving the fundraising team, finance team, and field team?

Is information shared about fundraising and field ministry successes, challenges and failures open and transparent both inside and outside the organization?

Do the fundraising, marketing, and communications departments share mutual goals, support one another and celebrate together?

Does the whole fundraising team, no matter the position, share the fundraising goals, have knowledge about campaigns, and participate in planning processes?

NO ————————|————————|————————|————————|———————— YES

PERHAPS BY THE TIME YOU CAME to the end of this list, you created a mental list of why moving towards the right of the continuum of many of these cultural indicators won't work in your global ministry. You may be concerned that your field team leaders have too many other priorities. Maybe you believe your board members will resist culture changes. Perhaps you do not believe other departments will share responsibility for fundraising goals. It could be that others think the development department is already overfunded. Maybe you have these concerns and more or others!

Addressing Internal Challenges

Several internal challenges often need to be addressed first to significantly improve outcomes down the road. Start with finding ways to help your development director nurture good communication and trust with both your CEO your CFO. Cultivate team building and collaboration between fundraising, communication, marketing and program staff. Find ways to retain fundraising staff, including the development director, for longer beginning with setting clear and realistic income expectations. Create realistic portfolio sizes so development officers can build deep relationships with donors and deliver customized communication to them. Shift your means of measuring fundraisers' individual successes so that competition is reduced and credit for gifts is shared.

The good news is that most of these priorities can be owned by leaders within development, marketing, and communications. Once these departments shift their internal culture, then new cultural priorities can be established in other areas of the minis-

Donors want to invest in a healthy philanthropic culture.

try. They take notice and become willing to engage with further cultural change.

Building connections with field staff is also essential. You want the development team and field staff to participate together as a unified team. This takes effort to build mutually supportive and empathetic relationships. Get your fundraising leaders involved in field leadership meetings to deepen empathy and increase mutual understanding and respect.

Sending a resource specialist to the field to stay with a missionary family and meeting the whole program team is an even better investment of time and money. The development professional will leave the program with new friends and a greater understanding of the field context. And the next time the resource specialist reaches out to request the yearly statistics, he or she will be met with less resistance. It can also work the other way. When a field program family visit their home office and the marketing team joyfully invites them to share stories from their personal experience, relationships strengthen, and the organization becomes more unified.

Changing Your Culture Brings Rewards

Shifting the culture is hard work, but the payoffs are huge for the whole organization. Donors want to invest in a healthy philanthropic culture. Over a five to seven-year period while I was working with the global missions organization I mentioned at the beginning of this chapter, I experienced the difference this can make first hand. We made many organizational changes and achieved our goal of creating a philanthropic culture. Donors went from only having relationships with development staff to becoming part of our organizational family. Deep and long-lasting friendships were forged between field missionary staff development staff and marketing staff. The team became willing to spend time together, serve one another, and pray for each other's needs.

Now, I assess organizational culture for many of my consulting clients and coach them on a roadmap forward. While each organization is different, I find that they can incrementally grow a culture of philanthropy. My hope for you as you move forward is that you would find joy in that journey!

BARBARA BOWMAN holds a bachelor of science degree in guidance and counseling with an emphasis in career management from Colorado Mesa University. She has more than thirty years of experience in nonprofit management and corporate career management including nine years as the vice president of advancement for a US$46 million global faith-based nonprofit. She and her husband live in Boise, Idaho. They have two adult children.

Chapter Reflections

- What weaknesses can you easily identify as your organization's current culture of philanthropy?
- What would it take to make small, incremental steps towards a healthy culture of philanthropy?
- What pay-off would your organization experience if it developed a healthy culture of philanthropy?
- How can you engage your board and/or executive team in the process of developing a culture of philanthropy?

Bibliography and Additional Resources

Evelyn and Walter Haas, Jr. Fund. "UnderDeveloped." Last updated January 14, 2013. https://www.haasjr.org/resources/underdeveloped.

Gibson, Cynthia M. "Beyond Fundraising: What Does It Mean to Build a Culture of Philanthropy?" Evelyn and Walter Haas, Jr. Fund, https://www.haasjr.org/sites/default/files/resources/Haas_CultureofPhilanthropy_F1_0.pdf.

Kanter, Beth, Anne Wallestad, Linda Wood, Katrina VanHuss, Andrea McManus, Jann Schultz, Cheryl Contee, Wendy Watson-Hallowell, Pamela Barden, and Russell Pomeranz. *Fundraising Matters: Building a Culture of Philanthropy*. Blackbaud Institute, 2017. https://institute.blackbaud.com/asset/npexperts-2017-fundraising-matters-building-a-culture-of-philanthropy/.

Social Transformation Project. "Tools & Resources." http://stproject.org/resources/.

The Alford Group. "Culture of Philanthropy: Assessing the Culture in Your Organization." https://alford.com/wp-content/uploads/2014/09/Culture-of-Philanthropy-Assessment-Grid-Updated.pdf.

CHAPTER 2

Involving CEOs and Boards in Fundraising

By Kristen Shuler

IT WAS 6:55 IN THE MORNING. I sat in my car in front of a quaint German restaurant that doubled as a meat market and deli. In minutes my CEO, *Kevin,*[1] and one of our board members, *Shawn,* would arrive for a breakfast meeting with me. We planned to discuss ways that Shawn could introduce his friends to our ministry. With a notebook and prospect list in hand, I asked the Lord for the Holy Spirit to work during the meeting. As we entered the restaurant together, I could already tell Shawn was ready.

As our conversation about family and personal lives winded down, I transitioned us to a discussion about Shawn's prospect list. I pulled out the list of names that he previously shared with me and handed out copies to him and Kevin. The next half hour Shawn thoughtfully shared ideas for strategies to approach each listed person. Yet I sensed there was something more behind his words than just a strategic mind.

I asked him, "Why do you personally invest your time, talent and treasure into this ministry?"

Shawn stopped and pondered my questions. His countenance changed. He fought back tears. "I want more people to enter the

---

1 Names throughout this chapter have been changed to retain privacy.

Fundraising is spiritual work.

kingdom of heaven as a result of how I live my life," he replied.

"And what causes that motivation?" I asked.

He paused and then looked directly at Kevin and me. "My life has been so changed by the gospel of Jesus Christ. I want others to experience that same life change," he said.

This shifted the dialogue for all of us. Instead of only considering the best process for introducing the people on Shawn's list to our ministry, we began to think about how we could discover God's purposes for the unique gifts and passions each had. And Shawn focused on ways he could discern their heartbeats and see how the Lord is at work in their lives. It was clear that what Shawn wanted was for more of his colleagues and friends to find the joy of participating with God in his work.

Engaging Your CEOs and Board Members in Fundraising

Fundraising is spiritual work. Every follower of Jesus has the opportunity to join with the Lord and others on a journey of faith and obedience under God's leading. When you allow God to shape and mold you into his image, you become one of his ambassadors carrying out his work as you give him your *time*, your *talent*, and your *treasure*.

Acknowledging God's work in your life and then coming alongside others in their journey becomes the foundation for your connection with others in the adventure of fundraising. Working with your CEOs and board members allows you to leverage the influence of relationships to catalyze the work of God in each of our lives: "... that he who began a good work in you will bring it to completion at the day of Jesus Christ" (Philippians 1:6, ESV).

According to a recent study[2] of over 2,700 executive and development directors, more than one in four admitted they either have no fundraising competency or are novices. The study further indicated that three out of four executive directors believe their board members do not do enough to support organizational fundraising.

As development professionals, you must cast a vision for fundraising to your CEOs and board members and then adequately equip them to successfully fulfill this responsibility. If you are your organization's CEO and development officer, you'll need to capture the vision for this responsibility yourself and then share it with your board.

Everyone knows leadership engagement in fundraising is critical. But why should *they* want to help with fundraising? It's hard work after all. Every organization must answer this question in their own way. However, vision and relationships form common and powerful foundational principles.

Sharing Vision and Making the Most of Relationships

CEOs and board members need a shared vision of the future and how they will participate in realizing that future. For example, if you want to see people motivated toward generosity for kingdom advancement, then you need your CEO and board members to catch this vision and make it their own. You must take an active role in helping them see their part.

But this responsibility does not fall solely on leadership. A primary duty of a chief development officer is to create a philanthropy culture among all staff and leadership – a culture in which each person participates in fundraising. Within that framework, CEOs and board members own the responsibility of fundraising and lead the organization toward full funding and fulfilling the

2 "UnderDeveloped." (2013, January). Reset Fundraising Curated Collection. https://www.haasjr.org/resources/underdeveloped

organization's mission. When this works successfully, vision is cultivated among the whole staff, and they each take part by encouraging generosity in their own networks.

But vision is just one part. Another significant lever for catalyzing a successful fundraising program is engaging your leadership's exclusive networks. Some prospects or donors will only meet with your CEO. In these cases, and in organizations that have development staff, the development officer manages donor relationships and the strategy for soliciting funds but requests that the CEO joins for meetings or sends personal communications.

The influence of your CEO should be embraced and leveraged in ways that honor a donor's time and expectations as well as the CEO's time. This is an important approach to consider not only for individuals but also for institutional donors. Often times, a foundation wants to hear the vision and the opportunity for supporting a project directly from the CEO. Know your audiences and leverage your CEO's influence accordingly.

For board members, peer-to-peer fundraising can yield greater new donor acquisition results than other models. The value of their relationships and the trust they have developed with colleagues and friends over time far exceeds other acquisition activities such as events, email campaigns, and social strategies. You want board members to identify those in their networks they can influence and invite them to learn more about your organization. Help them understand the power of their relational influence, and provide clear, simple opportunities for them to engage their networks.

Leveraging Leadership Influence

CEOs and board members that capture a vision for their part in fundraising efforts are a tremendous resource. To leverage this resource well, examine fundraising activities that fit your CEO and board members best and then prepare them for the work.

Start with your CEO. A CEO can both manage their own donor

The influence of your CEO should be embraced and leveraged in ways that honor a donor's time and expectations as well as the CEO's time.

caseload and support the whole team's fundraising activities. As you consider your database of existing and prospective donors, determine which need to be assigned to the CEO's caseload. Depending on the size of your organization, this can be anywhere from ten to fifty accounts. If your organization is small, your CEO needs to manage more accounts. Assign donors who prefer to connect with your CEO (i.e. CEOs of companies and board members) as well as your prospects with the highest giving capacity. If you have few or no fundraising staff, other leaders in your organization can also manage small donor caseloads.

Your CEO can support your team's fundraising efforts in several other key ways. Your CEO's influence can go a long way to support other fundraising team members' work with their caseloads. For example, your CEO can go with a leader or gift officer when they make their first ask to a donor after many months of cultivating a relationship with them. The CEO's presence in a meeting like this demonstrates your organization's value for a donor relationship.

Your CEO can use his or her influence in other ways, too, including hand signing gift acknowledgment letters, writing thank you letters for gifts over a certain amount, calling donors to thank them for gifts above a specified threshold, and contacting donors for milestone acknowledgments. Evaluate your CEO's available time to offer this kind of support before assigning tasks. You will set him or her up for failure if the volume of work is not achievable. Start slow and add new opportunities as your CEO masters his or her first few assignments.

Like your CEOs, your board members' time and influence can also support fundraising. Primarily, you want to provide your board members with ways they can introduce their networks to your ministry that match their available time.

One simple way board members can engage is to email introductions to their networks encouraging them to meet with the development director and/or CEO or attend an upcoming ministry event. Board members with more time could host a table at an event or go to a lunch meeting with the development director and/or CEO and someone in their network where they share more about your organization.

You could ask board members with flexibility to open their home to host a gathering of their friends to meet and hear from the development director and CEO about your ministry. Responsibilities like sending invitations, food, audio/visual requirements, and managing RSVPs can be managed by the development department or administrative staff to reduce a board member's burden for the event. In this way, your staff can create an easy path for a board member's generous gift of relational connections.

Setting CEOs and Board Members Up for Fundraising Success

As you identify various ways you can engage leadership to support fundraising efforts, remember that they need to be equipped for success. CEOs are greatly supported by administrative help managing their caseload. Ideally, a development director would help with the strategic activities, but in smaller organizations, an administrative assistant can fully support a CEO with all fundraising responsibilities.

Helping your CEO manage their caseload begins with creating action plans for each donor account. Each plan should have gift projections and a clear multi-step process including details of touch points culminating with an ask. Gift projections enable you

The best way to equip board members for fundraising is to regularly share stories about what God is doing through your ministry.

to prioritize your CEO's caseload so attention can first be given to those with higher giving potential. This prioritized list streamlines administrative tasks like scheduling donor meetings and executing other touch points from the action plan (i.e. mailing resources, writing thank you notes, making phone calls, etc.).

When a meeting occurs, the CEO should be equipped with a donor brief and materials to share with the donor. A donor brief can include giving history, notes from previous meetings, wealth capacity information, giving/project interests, and other research details. Also make sure your CEO has materials to update a donor on your ministry or make an ask. Finally, put systems in place to document the outcomes or action steps from the CEO's donor meetings to ensure follow through is properly managed and to help facilitate discussion for future meetings with each donor.

The best way to equip board members for fundraising is to regularly share quality stories and updates with them about what God is doing through your ministry. This grows their passion for what you do and naturally leads them to connect your ministry with their networks.

To simplify board fundraising involvement, create a *toolkit* for each board member activity. For example, if you want board members to invite people in their networks to an introductory lunch with your development director and/or CEO, a toolkit should include your expectations for their role in establishing a connection, participating in a lunch meeting and following-up with the prospect after the meeting. Give them a script for a phone call or text for an email they can use to invite people to a lunch meeting. You'll want to give them talking points they can use to share about your ministry with their contacts during the lunch meeting as well as in any other setting.

When your board expresses willingness and even enthusiasm to support fundraising efforts, it is critical to create a path for your board members to be successful. As a board member once said to me, "You just tell me what to do and how to do it, and I'll salute!"

As your CEO and board members experience success with fundraising, creatively celebrate their impact. Share these successes with whole board to both encourage those who provided assistance and to inspire others to catch a vision for how they, too, can support fundraising work.

Conclusion

Fundraising provides an opportunity to invite others to participate in God's work through your ministry. It is a privilege to be charged with the responsibility to raise funds and to empower others to do the same. Seek to understand why your leadership is so impassioned by your ministry, give them a clear vision for their involvement in fundraising, and then equip them to find success in their efforts. Not only will the responsibility of fundraising be distributed among more passionate advocates for your ministry, but, like Shawn, they will also discover its joy!

KRISTEN SHULER serves as the executive vice president of development at East-West Ministries International (www.eastwest.org). Prior to joining East-West, Kristen primarily served in evangelism and church planting strategies across South America. At East-West, Kristen continues to fulfill her call to missions by motivating hearts toward generosity for kingdom advancement.

Chapter Reflections

- When will you next cast vision to your CEO and/or board members for supporting your organization's fundraising efforts? How will you encourage them to help fulfill your organization's mission by getting involved with fundraising?
- What are two to three practical ways you can better equip your CEO to support your organization's fundraising efforts?
- Identify two to three board members who would be most willing to support your fundraising efforts. After casting vision for their involvement in fundraising and asking them to take practical steps toward supporting your fundraising work, what will be your next step to engage each in fundraising?

Bibliography and Additional Resources

Rodin, R. Scott. *The Third Conversion: a Novelette*. Colbert, WA: Kingdom Life, 2015.

Rodin, Scott. "How Much Is Enough?" Produced by ECFA. *Excellence in Ministry*, May 1, 2019. MP3 Audio. https:// excellenceinministry.podbean.com/e/how-much-is-enough-scott-rodin/.

CHAPTER 3

Building a Fundraising Team from Scratch

By Nathan Burns

HIRING YOUR NONPROFIT'S FIRST FUNDRAISER IS quite a challenging proposition. A lot rides on who you pick and then how you work together to create a fundraising plan and build the team needed to sustain your fundraising model long-term. If you are at this point, you and your board of directors are confronting a core question – how do you find funding to expand and make a bigger impact? This is a vital moment in determining the future of your good work.

First, you face a *catch 22*. To increase funding for your nonprofit, you will want to hire a fundraiser. But hiring someone means that you need even more money than before! And you want a person who will be really good, right? To escape this *catch 22*, your new hire must at least raise what you need and cover the cost of their salary!

Your second challenge is what sort of person do you need? Many nonprofit leaders find themselves evaluating two general directions. Option A: hiring someone who is untested but doesn't require a high salary. Or option B: seeking out someone who has a proven record or stellar personality but requires a greater salary. But which is the best route? In option A, you might mitigate financial risk but fail to really make a decisive difference. Pursue option B, and you might hire someone who is expensive and really not a fit for your mission.

These challenges are just your first obstacles! It is not easy, but what nonprofit has ever scaled its programs without tending to its "economic engine?"[1] This is vital to sustaining the mission you are so passionate about and it can be tremendously rewarding.[2]

If hiring a fundraiser and building a development team is in your future, here is the best advice I can give you – don't tackle it on your own. In this chapter, I introduce key questions you need to consider that help you begin to map out a plan for building a fundraising team from scratch. But as Proverbs says, plans fail for lack of advisors.[3] Get your board involved in relentlessly tracking down and pursuing anyone else who might have the knowledge, wisdom, or connections you need. After forming your circle of advisors, you might even want to share this chapter with them in order to gauge whether or not you are all on the same page.

Where Is Your Low Hanging Fruit?

Before you make a plan for who to hire and your strategy for building a fundraising team, you need to understand your context. Here is the big question to start – where is your *low hanging fruit*? Put another way – where will new, intentional fundraising efforts most likely yield the greatest return in the next twelve months?

There are many common strategies you can employ in fundraising. For example, you can host events, do email blasts, mail letters, launch crowdfunding and digital campaigns, seek corporate and foundation grants, or build one-on-one relationships

---

1 James C. Collins, *Good to Great and the Social Sectors Why Business Thinking Is Not the Answer* (Auckland, N.Z.: Royal New Zealand Foundation of the Blind, 2012).

2 Leslie R. Crutchfield and Heather McLeod Grant, *Forces for Good: The Six Practices of High-Impact Nonprofits* (Jossey Bass Inc, 2012).

3 Proverbs 15:22.

Before you make a plan for who to hire and your strategy for building a fundraising team, you need to understand your context.

with individuals who can give major gifts. But what are *your* top three strategies?

Knowing *your* context well helps you discern what skill set your new hire needs. It's important to note, though, that at the core, all fundraising strategies involve cultivating relationships with individuals.[4] A bedrock truism is that "people give to people." That is why the best choice for your first hire is usually someone who is a naturally gifted relationship builder.

Are you beginning to get a picture of who you might hire? But finding a person is only the beginning. You also need to look at how to set up your new hire for success. Let's get more specific in probing for low hanging fruit. Consider these questions:

- How is your nonprofit currently raising the most money? Is it at an event, through letters, or something else?
- What fundraising method or focus do you think could bring in a greater return, and how does this compare to what you are already doing?
- Considering your answers above, would a new hire be able help you generate enough income in their first twelve months to satisfy you? Would you be willing to give them another twelve months after that to try to really increase your financial base?

---

4 Steve Thomas, *Donoricity: Raise More Money for Your Nonprofit with Strategies Your Donors Crave* (Austin, TX: Lioncrest Publishing, 2017).

You may not have full answers to each question. That's okay! But these questions are important, so continue to ponder them.

It doesn't make any sense to hire a new fundraiser without having a roadmap to success. It takes a whole year for someone to learn about your nonprofit. Yes, such lead time can be scary, but it makes sense. In major gifts fundraising (i.e., developing relationships with individuals who can give large gifts, like $10,000 or more), it takes eighteen to twenty-four months of relationship building to get a major gift.[5] Your best donors develop from ongoing relational involvement.[6]

Strong fundraising programs develop gradually. That is why you need to get started now. Let me share examples with you of how others began. As you read each case see how they reviewed their context, created a basic road map for success, and started on the hard work of increasing their nonprofit's impact through fundraising.

Case One: The Local Start-Up Nonprofit

When I was a local nonprofit board member, we realized that fundraising events were a good way for our organization to develop initial support and attract both volunteers and donors. The nonprofit was so young that we couldn't hire a fundraiser yet, so we added a board member who had experience with events. This strategy worked well in the early years. Eventually, we realized we could expand our ministry. As our board discussed "low hanging fruit" we realized focusing on building relationships with churches and high-capacity donors was our next step. Our events drew both groups, but someone needed to cultivate those relationships

5 Richard Perry and Jeff Schriefels, "How Long Does It Take to Start a Major Gift Program?" *Veritus Group*, September 27, 2017, https://veritusgroup.com/takes-long-time-start-major-gift-program/.

6 Eric Foley, *Coach Your Champions: the Transformational Giving Approach to Major Donor Fundraising* (Colorado Springs, CO: .W Publishing, 2009).

all year long. So we hired a fundraiser with years of experience and a good personal network in the local community.

Case Two: The Nonprofit Built on a Self-Support Fundraising Model

An international nonprofit had decades of success built on a self-support model: most staff cultivated partnerships with donors who funded their salaries and a portion of their business expenses. This model gave this nonprofit a great support base and a strong reputation which presented an opportunity to develop gifts from foundations. When they established their first sizable fundraising team, they hired a development director gifted in building personal relationships with foundation leaders. This director then focused on hiring staff experienced in writing grant proposals and administering grants.

Case Three: The Nonprofit Needing to Expand a Major Gifts Program

The nonprofit that I currently serve needed to start a nation-wide major gifts program. But you can't just parachute a fundraiser into a location and expect them to succeed. I had to look for low hanging fruit. After reviewing the available data, searching for "bright spots," seeking the counsel of others, and spending a good amount of time in prayer, it become clear that we needed to start in Texas.[7] Still, we didn't have a lot of current donors there.

An individual hired to cultivate donors for us in Texas would be starting a "new territory." We needed to get every other variable under our control to ensure success. It was an answer to prayer when I met someone naturally extroverted with analogous sales and ministry experience who had a deep personal network

---

7 Chip Heath and Dan Heath, *Switch: How to Change Things When Change Is Hard* (London: Random House, 2011).

You need to find a way to hire people of character and passion while paying a reasonable salary.

in Dallas, Texas. In the first year, this colleague raised almost his full salary, and in year two, he raised twice that amount!

In each example, a person was hired who could seize upon identified opportunities. Each hire was a highly relational person. Those gifted in administration were either in the organization already or hired after initial success. If you proceed this way, you are on a good path.

Finding the Right Person to Hire

Beware of two pitfalls. Remember at the beginning that I mentioned the challenges of hiring an experienced fundraiser and finding a way to afford them? Simultaneously, you need to find a way to hire people of character and passion while paying a reasonable salary.

Fundraising is tough, and a fundraiser's passion and character must drive them to move forward and persevere. It is not enough to just be a professional – especially in a faith-based nonprofit. You must be motivated by moral commitment and a genuine enthusiasm for the cause. Otherwise, how can you inspire others to participate in it with you?

As you go through a hiring process, you will need to discern each candidate's character. Does the person in front of you exhibit the characteristics of a servant leader? Humility is the litmus test. Those without humility will not make good partners.[8] They

---

8 Patrick Lencioni, *The Ideal Team Player: How to Recognize and Cultivate the Three Essential Virtues: a Leadership Fable* (New Delhi, India: Wiley India, 2018).

will not help create a culture of community on your team.[9] They will also not be able to authentically serve your donors.

You may have noticed that I did not say that the person you hire needs to be an expert in your mission. Knowledge can be taught, and experts/insiders often have a "curse of knowledge" that limits their effectiveness as champions for your cause.[10]

If you are going to hire someone of character, someone humble that you can depend on, and someone with the passion to sacrifice to make your mission a success, then the truth is that you need to pay them properly. Listen, I've hired fundraisers. I know it is hard. There is rarely enough funding in the nonprofit world. Nonprofit salaries are already below those of the for-profit world. And even in the nonprofit world, it can be hard to compete with those at the top of compensation surveys for your niche. Here is what I urge you to do:

Pay a Salary and Don't Offer Commission

Commissions are a great tool in the for-profit world, but they create ethical dilemmas in the nonprofit space. Donors give toward a certain charitable purpose, not to the fundraiser's salary. Also, the fundraiser's primary motivation should be passion, not for their salary. Finally, great fundraising is based on philanthropic partnership, not on transactional giving.[11] For these reasons, it is unethical in the nonprofit space to offer a commission to fundraisers.[12]

---

9 Mark Miller, *The Secret of Teams: What Great Teams Know and Do* (San Francisco: Berrett-Koehler Publishers, 2011).

10 Thomas, *Donoricity*.

11 R. Scott Rodin and Gary G. Hoag, *The Sower: Redefining the Ministry of Raising Kingdom Resources* (Winchester, VA: ECFA Press, 2010).

12 "ECFA Standard 7.5 – Stewardship of Charitable Gifts: Percentage Compensation for Securing Charitable Gifts," ECFA, accessed June 30, 2020, https://www.ecfa.org/Content/Comment75.

Focus less on the salary and more on how to get a good return.

Don't Require Your Fundraiser to Raise Their Own Support

Many nonprofits in the Christian space have successfully used a self-support model for most of their staff. But making full-time fundraisers raise their own support creates conflicts of interest. Should a donor give to the organization or to the fundraiser's own support? If a fundraiser is hurting for support, getting a new personal supporter ensures they are around to help with fundraising next year. On the other hand, what if the nonprofit can't hit its organizational fundraising goals? Should the fundraiser keep their job because they are fully supported even though they can't raise enough for the organization? Or should they be let go even though they aren't costing the organization anything?

Once a fundraiser hits his or her stride, they should bring in four to ten times their cost. I'd take that return on investment any day! Focus less on the salary and more on how to get a good return. Let's come back to that old *catch 22* – you need a fundraiser because you need more money, but they will cost you money. Do you have doubts or anxieties about the risk of hiring someone who will cost so much? Or are you facing the hard reality that you just don't have the funds right now?

Hiring a Fundraiser Is a Worthy Investment

Here is the question to ask yourself and anyone else facing mental and emotional obstacles to moving forward – have we truly understood the full cost of our mission? Haven't you just said that the cost of the future of your mission includes the cost of a fundraiser's salary? If so – that is the key to your way forward. A fundraiser isn't a necessary evil. They are an integral part of the mission, and the cost of hiring them is the cost of actually creating a sustainable resource engine that can keep your mission thriving. Why wouldn't you want to invest in that?

Fundraising is an essential part of your mission. Yes, people want to make sure you don't spend too much, because we expect nonprofits to be thrifty. But that concern is secondary to accomplishing your mission. It's not hard to convince others that you need to have a fundraiser. People in business understand that you have to build a sales team to succeed. In fact, if you don't have the money to hire a fundraiser, you may have actually just found your first fundraising priority!

Let's make this concrete. Suppose your mission is positioned to expand. You want to launch a $300,000 campaign to support your expansion. You know that your current donors could probably provide the first $100,000. After that, you need someone to raise the remaining $200,000 over the next two years. If you don't hire someone to help you, you are fairly sure that the campaign will fail.

Consider this: Why not add the cost of the new fundraiser into the campaign? This would allow you to direct all your initial donations toward your hire. Let's say that this new position's salary, benefits, and miscellaneous costs (travel, meals, computer, etc.) totaled around $100,000. You know your campaign isn't going to succeed without a person on board filling this position. Why not make your $300,000 campaign into a $400,000 campaign with the first $100,000 raised going toward the new fundraiser? Such a decision could even strengthen your proposition to donors. You can explain to them that you are building the campaign in such a way that you'll have the fundraising capacity at the end to support the higher ongoing costs that come with expansion.

You could go to current donors – the group who could provide the first $100,000 – and share how their investment would ensure your long-term success. Their $100,000 would bring a new fundraiser on board, and then that person would raise another

$100,000 in their first twelve months, and $200,000 in the next year. That's a total of $400,000! If all went as planned, you would end this campaign fully funded and have a fundraiser on staff who is poised to raise $300,000 in year three.

What if you are stuck?

Alright, let's get totally serious – if you still can't see a way to afford a fundraiser, what should you do? It rarely works to take half measures like having a current staff member split time 50/50 on fundraising and program work, hiring someone part-time, or hiring someone full-time but making them raise their personal support. You may fail when you hire someone full-time. But you are almost sure to fail if you take half measures. So why try this again and again? Sometimes it is because you believe you have no other choice. But you do have another option.

Go back to your board. The top leadership of your nonprofit deserves a chance to see the realities involved in starting a fundraising team. If they choose to engage, board members have capacity to help you find people who have answers. Boards must be given the opportunity to choose a way forward.

If your board is unable to help, or chooses passivity, you are in a bad position. I witnessed a Christian seminary on the brink who couldn't reckon with this. They slowly failed. I saw another nonprofit start-up fail primarily because the board could not build momentum in fundraising. And I served on a board where all the members resigned when they realized the hard changes needed! The upshot is this – if you can't hire a fundraiser and your board won't help, then your problem may be more of a board issue.

This Work Is Worth Doing

Friend, at the start of this chapter, I warned you there would be challenges ahead. Now you know what those challenges are. I hope you now feel equipped to cope. Imagine what can happen if you succeed! This is work worth doing even if it means difficult conversations. Imagine if enough of your board and nonprofit leadership get behind you?! That is a future worth praying for and enduring to see come about.

NATHAN BURNS is the vice president of advancement for Pioneers, a mission agency he's served with since 2010. He has a master's in international studies. He and his wife have two young children, and together, they have been deeply involved in a Central Florida ministry that aids trafficked women. He has experience serving on two different nonprofit boards.

Chapter Reflections

- What were your answers to the three questions asked at the beginning of this chapter?
- What is your biggest challenge in finding the right person to build your fundraising team? Who could help you create a plan to overcome it?
- How has your board supported efforts to build your fundraising team? What steps could you take to build stronger relationships with leadership in your organization that will improve their support?

Bibliography and Additional Resources

Collins, Jim. *Good to Great and the Social Sectors: Why Business Thinking is Not the Answer*. HarperCollins, 2005. This book will help you understand how a nonprofit runs and where fundraising fits into its economic engine.

Crutchfield, Leslie. *Forces for Good: The Six Practices of High-Impact Nonprofits*. John Wiley & Sons, 2009. Review the case studies to learn more about successful nonprofits.

Foley, Eric. *Coach Your Champions: The Transformational Giving Approach to Major Donor Fundraising*. .W Publishing, 2010. This book offers specific guidance on building a major gifts program.

Lencioni, Patrick M. *The Ideal Team Player: How to Recognize and Cultivate the Three Essential Virtues*. Jossey-Bass, 2016.

Miller, Mark. *The Secret of Teams: What Great Teams Know and Do*. Berrett-Koehler Publishers, 2011.

Mission Increase. https://www.mif.org/. This organization has helpful resources for learning more about fundraising and training courses that may be useful for new fundraising hires.

The Chronicle of Philanthropy. https://www.philanthropy.com/.
Purchase a subscription to this periodical to stay up on
nonprofit fundraising trends and gain access to their
webinars and toolboxes.

Thomas, Steve. *Donoricity: Raise More Money for Your Nonprofit
with Strategies Your Donors Crave.* Lioncrest Publishing,
2018. This book explains how to craft fundraising messages.

Veritus Group. "Passionate Giving Blog™". https://veritusgroup.
com/passionate-giving-blog/. This blog offers insights in
fundraising and major gifts fundraising in particular.

CHAPTER 4

Crafting an Exceptional Grant Proposal

By David Broussard

IN 2013, I WAS THE GRANTS and research officer for a five-hospital healthcare system. One day, I received an invitation to participate in a system-wide redesign of the accounting software. The accounting team had discovered a *grants* module in the new software package, and because they knew my team "got grants," they called me. They said this software package would more seamlessly integrate our grant revenue tracking with the overall healthcare system's accounting – a problem that we identified in the past.

I showed up to the week-long training to learn about the grants module only to discover that it was a grants *accounting* module. While it would be a useful tool for a grant accountant, it was not designed for a grant manager or a grant writer like me. In the end, despite the software debacle, the accountants and I all became good friends.

As in the situation above, just because a person uses the words *grant* and *grant proposal* doesn't mean he or she has the same understanding of those terms! These definitions and the framework in which they are used are critical to write proposals that will be best positioned to be funded. Quality written communication skills (clarity, good grammar and punctuation, etc.) are an

The first step in knowing your audience is researching the *history* or origin of the grant making organization.

essential part of an organization's ability to produce proposals; however, producing good *grant* proposals also requires a specialized lens and perspective. This begins with adequately defining the purpose and context of grants and grant making.

Grants and Grant Makers

Unfortunately, many people identify any funding from a foundation as a *grant*. This frequently leads ministries to believe that their organization is receiving grants. But just because funding comes from a foundation, doesn't mean it is a grant. Some foundations are simply *philanthropic checkbooks* for a couple or a family. They have no requirements, no application, and essentially behave like a major gift donor. They make *gifts* and not *grants*.

Grants require a formal request and obligate the grantee to a different level of accountability and reporting. If your organization receives unrestricted funding from a foundation, it is a gift. Grants, however, can only be used for a specific program or project with its own budget and outcomes. So, creating a grant proposal is not the same as making a request for a gift.

If you are seeking a grant from institutional funders, then you will need to submit a well-defined application form or proposal following specific guidelines to a group of decision-makers. They then vote on whether or not to fund your organization's request. These *grant makers* include foundations, public charities (US – 501(c)(3) nonprofits) that raise and then redistribute funds through an application process, or other legal corporations with a competitive grant awards process.

To secure a grant, your request will need to stand out from the rest. So, what are steps can you take to create a winning grant proposal?

Step One: Know Your Audience

You have likely heard some version of the *spray and pray* method of proposal writing. Using a direct mail strategy, in this method you send the same request for funding to dozens, if not hundreds, of grant makers. Given the difference between grants and gifts (and major donors and grant makers), you can see why this approach doesn't work. It also neglects the first necessary step in the process: researching your audience.

If your organization is going to ask a group of decision makers for a restricted gift for a project, then knowing who the decision makers are and the structure in which they operate is mission critical. You can't write for an audience you don't know.

So, who are these grant makers?

Every foundation is different. There is no a standard one-size-fits-all formula in grant writing. Therefore, the first step in knowing your audience is researching the history or origin of the grant making organization. Consider the following questions:

- How did the organization come to be?
- Who were the founders?
- Why did they start it?
- What was important to them?

Grant making entities start for a reason. I know one foundation that reads the original charter of their founding at every board meeting to keep them rooted in the founder's purpose and intent. Sometimes, you can also find foundation websites with more information about their history than their actual grant application process. If the grant makers are sending out a message, effective grant seekers need to listen.

Knowing your audience also means learning about who manages the grant making organization. Who stewards the grant maker's resources and votes on decisions to award funds? Find ways to appropriately link your grant seeking organization with a grant maker's board. That does not mean you can immediately approach a board member to ask for funding. Rules often govern how board members interact with potential grantees. Sometimes, board members are encouraged to submit organizations and projects to be considered for funding. Other times they are actually banned from doing so. But talking to a board member about the foundation's process is almost always acceptable. Building a relationship between your organization and a decision maker will benefit you as you write your proposal.

Next, learn the grant maker's process for receiving grant requests. It is essential to be aware of how the board and staff make funding decisions – their operational structures and request pathways. Sometimes your proposal is the last step in a long process that includes months or even years of effort to engage funders. Other times, a proposal is the first step to begin a dialogue with a funder. Grant writers need to know how much information, in what order, and what kind of background and context is needed in a proposal.

You can request this information by calling the funder or visiting their website. Many private foundations list it in Part XV on their 990-PF (a private foundation's US tax return). They give details in this section about how they make contributions. It reads as follows:

> Check here if the foundation only makes contributions to preselected charitable organizations and does not accept unsolicited requests for funds. *If the foundation makes gifts, grants, etc. to individuals or organizations under other conditions, complete items 2a, b, c, and d.* (italics added)

Items 2a, b, c, and d could ask interested parties to call the foundation's offices, send an email, send a letter of inquiry (which is a short resume of your organization and the project for which you would be requesting funding), or even a full proposal. Addendums to the 990-PF may further explain how the foundation accepts grant requests (or not). These processes guide the format of each step of communication with the foundation. So, if a foundation provides this guidance, follow it. It is not advisable to send a full proposal to a foundation without an invitation or clear direction from them asking you to do so.

Variations in the history, board, and process of each foundation will result in very different proposals. If you want your proposal to be reviewed and accepted, research each funder to understand their specific guidelines, restrictions, requirements, and process.

Finally, grant makers are not faceless, sterile entities. Grant makers are made up of normal people who have good days and bad days like everyone else. Highs and lows in the markets can affect their investments. Leadership changes, including when an executive director moves on or a founding couple passes away, can impact staff morale. A program officer who was once your advocate could leave for another position and someone who doesn't know your organization could replace them. So be aware of the dynamic nature of an institutional funder's makeup and evolution as you prepare the content of your proposal and time its submission.

Step Two: Accept the Universal Rule

Once a grant seeking organization knows who the grant maker is, then they must learn the universal rule that applies to institutional funders: making "good grants." That looks different for each funder, but with careful study you can discover ways to craft a proposal that demonstrates how an investment in your nonprofit will be a good grant.

One of my colleagues said that his goal was to help organizations become ones that "foundations love to grant to." When a grant maker favors a nonprofit, they can't wait to get the next report and proposal so they can continue supporting that organization's work. That happens when grant professionals to do their research and honestly evaluate whether or not an organization will be a good fit for the grant maker.

So, what is a good grant? It is a financial investment that accomplishes what a foundation intends it to accomplish. In other words, a grant maker doesn't give donations; they buy outcomes. So, if you want to produce a stellar grant proposal for your organization, you must take into account both who the funder is and what they are trying to *buy*.

If the foundation has any kind of staff or management, talk with them about this aspect of their grant making. But if you can't have a conversation with a funder, look at which organizations the grant maker has previously funded. To learn more about what this funder loves to support, research their top three grant recipients over the last three to five years.

Equipped with the knowledge about who the funder is and what they love to support, you can now proceed to the last step before writing your proposal.

Step Three: Understand What You Can Measure and Why It's Important

If grant makers want to buy outcomes that align with their mission, grant seekers must be able to measure their outcomes. This is nonnegotiable. Grants require reporting. If an outcome can't be measured, it can't be reported.

If a foundation sends a check for $100,000 to an organization to carry out a year's worth of programming, it is not doing so in order for the organization to keep busy with activities. The purpose is to see an agreed upon *result* from those activities. If your organization can only report activities that happened without

A winning grant proposal clearly describes what you will be delivering to the funder.

outcomes, how will the foundation know their investment accomplished what it was given to do? Sadly, this happens frequently, and frustrated foundation boards are left shrugging their shoulders and hoping that God blesses the work.

A winning grant proposal clearly describes what you will be delivering to the funder. If grantors are buying outcomes that align with their mission, then grant seeking organizations need to understand if they are able to deliver those outcomes or not. Knowing what an organization is doing (activities and outputs), why it's important (clarity of vision), and demonstrating how their work makes a difference (outcomes and impact), provides the elements needed to create a proposal that is more compelling than the majority that grant makers receive.

Unfortunately, many organizations struggle to adequately express their "impact" or explain how they participate in bringing transformation to those they serve. To more clearly demonstrate this, they need a theory of change: a map that shows the logical progression of inputs, activities, outputs, and outcomes that organizations use to bring about a long-term change. Experts can help organizations develop theories of change and other tools to evaluate outcomes. If your organization does not have funds to hire someone, free online resources can also get you started. Moving in this direction will require an investment of time and money, humility to listen to recommendations, and a willingness to shift organizational culture to accommodate new procedures.

Begin with a logic model – a diagram of program components that lead to your desired outcome. A simple one will allow internal staff and program managers to better define and explain how

Write everything in your full proposal as if it is a legally binding contract.

their work flows into the accomplishment of the organization's mission and vision. Logic models also reveal program misalignment or *gaps* in logic. For example, if an organization's vision is to lift children out of poverty but the output from their activities is a Bible translated into the children's native language, a logic model will show that the solution to the problem doesn't match the organization's work. This presents an opportunity, before writing a full proposal, to go back and align your vision and activities which will give your organization the best chance for a long-term institutional funding relationship. Grant makers often require that proposals include a theory of change or a logic model, and even when it's not required, I don't know any grant maker that wouldn't appreciate one!

While funders don't expect an organization to measure everything and control all outcomes, they do expect the organization to know its programs well enough to show them what can and can't be measured. The work of step three is committing to measurable outcomes that can be reported to the foundation at the end of the grant period.

Step Four: Write Your Proposal

Grant writers begin their work by researching grant makers to gaining a full understanding of their context and vision. Then they consider how their own organization can help the funder *buy* the outcomes they desire. Once these steps are complete, writing the actual proposal goes fast and easy.

In his book, *The 7 Habits of Highly Effective People*, Stephen

Covey says to begin with the end in mind. As a grant writer, this should be your mantra. You need to constantly think about what and how you are going to report back to the funder. A grant maker may even provide you with a copy of their reporting requirements. If they don't, ask for them before beginning the proposal. This will help you to know the grant makers expectations and determine how to best describe your project.

Remember that you are not writing for mass marketing or for a fundraising appeal. My recommendation is to write everything in your full proposal as if it is a legally binding contract. Proposals need greater depth including details of delivered and evaluated results. Attention to measurements along with descriptions of a project's full impacts and outcomes should take up the majority of your allotted word count. Stories of impact or testimonies can be good additions, but if something has to be cut, cut the stories and not the program design and outcome reporting.

In addition to whatever requirements are contained in a grant application, consider the following questions to focus your proposal writing:

- What are you trying to do?
- Why does it matter?
- How will you know you're successful?
- Why are you best positioned to do it?

If your proposal answers these questions clearly and concisely, it is more likely to be funded.

Conclusion

Grant proposal writing is all about understanding the grant maker and the grant seeking organization's outcome measurements. When these two elements are solidly in place, an experienced grant professional will have no trouble presenting a concise and well-structure case that shows how an investment in the grant seeking organization will accomplish the vision of the funder. Arriving at this point requires the full commitment of leadership and program staff. Every area in an organization needs to be ready for a "deep dive" to create an exceptional proposal. If your grant seeking organizations isn't ready for this, a seasoned professional can be an indispensable asset to move you in the right direction.

Finally, being a writer does not mean you are a grant writer – just like I was a grant writer but wasn't a grant accountant! You likely know writers who write for promotion, direct mail, advertising, or for other fundraising materials, but that does not mean they can write grant proposals. In fact, many of them cringe at the idea. Finding an experienced grant professional can save you time, money, and sometimes your organization's reputation as you engage with institutional funders.

DAVID BROUSSARD is a certified grant professional (GPC) and has worked in nonprofit development since 1997. He is fluent in French and is the founder and president of Impact France (www.impactfrance.org) which has facilitated over $8.5 million in giving to national French ministries. He has a bachelor's degree in French from Dickinson College. He and his family live near Atlanta, Georgia.

Chapter Reflections

- What examples of grants versus gifts have you encountered in your own work?
- What is your organization's theory of change? If you do not have a theory of change, what steps will you take to create one? What challenges could creating one present and how can you overcome those challenges?

Bibliography and Additional Resources

Candid Learning. https://learning.candid.org/. This site offers free and paid grant courses and sessions.

Center for Theory of Change. https://www.theoryofchange.org/. Go to this site to learn more about theories of change and logic models.

Grant Professionals Association. https://grantprofessionals.org.

The Grantsmanship Center. https://tgci.com/. This site offers comprehensive, paid training.

CHAPTER 5

Conducting a Development Audit

By Michael VanHuis

EVERY ORGANIZATION IS ACCUSTOMED TO ANNUAL financial audits. This ever-daunting process looms upon finance departments like an annual physical from your doctor – you know you need to do it, but you nevertheless dread it. The reality is you need both, and when you get the report back from the CPA firm or your doctor, you are relieved to know the information they provide. It gives tangible next steps to improve. Annual audit process shouldn't only be for finances. Many areas of organizations would benefit from one.

For a while, I led the operations team at a mission agency. When issues surfaced in the human resource department, I realized that their policies and procedures had not been reviewed in years. As a result, we started an annual HR policies and procedures audit to refine and strengthen them to better support staff and future organizational growth.

After working as a major gifts officer, I coached mission agencies with fundraising and development. As I analyzed agencies, I realized that most had a vision for how much money they needed to raise but did not know if they could raise it. They would often hire a development director with the expectation that a magician would arrive on the scene and instantly raise all the money they

Many Christian nonprofits do not prepare in any way before hiring a development director.

thought they needed. When the new development director could not provide the magical amount of money, they were either fired or left frustrated.

When staff members don't reach the potential you dreamed they would, fault usually lies in two places. It may be with the employee. Perhaps he or she was not qualified, did not work diligently, or did not fit well with your team. The fault could also be with your organization – the employer. It could stem from poor management. However, another deeper and pervasive problem also exists. Many Christian nonprofits do not prepare in any way before hiring a development director.

Doing your homework means being able to answer basic questions. What is your organization's history, present work, and future vision? What is the working relationship between your CEO and board? How has fundraising and development functioned in the past? What place does fundraising have in your organization's culture? How are your CEO and board involved in fundraising? If you can't answer these questions, you will end up hiring people who will not fit your culture or achieve success in their work. You will handicap them before they start!

A fundraising and development audit is a practical way to improve. Consider doing one every year or at least prior to hiring a development officer. This chapter is designed to help you think about key focus areas for an audit like this. It will give you a framework to better understand who you are and what you need to do to solidify your fundraising foundation and build a stronger and healthier future.

Development Audit Key One: Donor Knowledge

Your organization should be able to pull donor data at any time. In fact, this data should be in a regular report or dashboard for the CEO and development team. This tool gives perspective on your organization's whole network of supporters and brings a critical reality check as you consider new initiatives and current ministry solubility. Consider the following questions:

DONOR QUANTITY: How many donors do you have?

- How many donors do you have this year?
- How does your current quantity of donors compare to each of the previous five years?
- How many give monthly, quarterly or annually?

DONOR PROFILES: What do know about your donors?

- What types of donors do you have – foundations, organizations, businesses, individuals?
- What is their capacity to give?
- What is their giving frequency (monthly, quarterly, annually)?
- What are their interests?
- Who are your lapsed donors?

GIFT DESIGNATIONS: What do your donors give to?

- To individuals on the field?
- To individuals in the home office?
- To a general fund for the organization?
- To field projects?
- To other special projects?

DONOR COMMUNICATION: How do you inform and connect with your donors?

- What materials about your organization do all donors receive?
- How are donors thanked?
- What information do donors receive at different donor thresholds?
- How are donors invited to engage in ways beyond giving?

DONOR ENGAGEMENT: How are your donors engaged in other ways with your organization?

- How many pray for your organization or staff?
- How many attend events?
- How many volunteer with your organization?
- In what other ways, besides giving, are donors engaged with your organization?

When your organization sets a huge financial goal without taking time to understand if your current donor base can meet it, you set the stage for failure. Relentlessly pursuing the same donors year after year without expanding your base fatigues your donors. An accurate understanding of your donor's capacities will also help you set your ask. This helps you prevent missing out on opportunities because you've asked too much or offending because you've asked too much. It also reveals who God has raised up to support the work that you are called to steward. This should increase your thankfulness for what God has done and increase your reliance on him to provide what is necessary for his work to continue.

Development Audit Key Two:
Past and Current Development Initiatives

Every organization has fundraising and development history. It may be small or substantial. It could be simple or sophisticated. What wins and losses occurred over those years? With what foundations have you engaged even if you are no longer connected to them? This paints a picture of what led you to your current point. Your areas for analysis here would include these items:

ENGAGING WITH FOUNDATIONS

- With which have you interacted?
- When was the last time you engaged with them?
- What have they given to?
- Have you ever researched other foundations that may be in your area or that may be interested in what you do?

ENGAGING WITH CURRENT STAFF (HOME AND FIELD) AND ALUMNI

- How many current staff give? How many alumni?
- How have you encouraged current and previous staff to give?
- How have you invited and equipped current and previous staff to share about organizational giving opportunities with their contacts?

ENGAGING WITH ALL DONORS THROUGH ELECTRONIC AND PRINT MAILINGS

- What kinds of mailings do donors receive in what formats and at what frequency? (Examples of mailings: receipts, newsletters, thank you letters, appeal letters)
- What are the main messages in these mailings and are the messages unified across different pieces and consistent with one another?
- Who represents your organization in these mailings?

ENGAGING NEW AND CURRENT DONORS THROUGH EVENTS

- What events have you done in the past at what frequency?
- What return on investment have you received from events?
- What follow-up steps have you taken with attendees?
- What feedback have you received from attendees?

ENGAGING THE WIDER PUBLIC ONLINE IN GIVING

- Do giving appeals appear regularly on your website and social media pages? Do these appeals yield a steady stream of new donors?
- How have you consistently reinforced the messages of your mailings on your website and social media pages?
- How easy or difficult is giving online?
- Have you ever gone through your own giving process as if you were a donor?

Information like this could save a new development officer months of time and potentially wasted effort. Understanding your past and present efforts helps you work more wisely in the future.

I once worked with an organization that was considering closing their doors. I asked how much money they would need to avoid shutting down decades of work among the unreached. They needed about $250,000 to remain soluble. When I asked them about approaching a foundation for funding, they said they could not remember the last time they'd done that. A foundation that previously gave them funds was only a couple of hours from their home office! That foundation gave generously to many organizations like theirs, but they failed to steward the relationship and ask. In fact, they forgot about the relationship. Imagine how different the story may have been if they reviewed this information annually and acted upon it?

Development Audit Key Three: Organizational Development Integration

How connected are development efforts across your organization? Is development work isolated or is it integrated with all of your essential teams? Each of these relationships should be audited for connectivity and partnership:

DEVELOPMENT AND COMMUNICATIONS

- Are development projects represented in what you communicate? If you are not asking, people do not know about potential giving options, and they will give to someone else.

DEVELOPMENT AND IT

- Can your development team access the data they need to appropriately engage with donors?

DEVELOPMENT AND CHURCH RELATIONS/PARTNERSHIPS

- Are churches engaged to deepen their giving to missionaries, projects and your organization?
- Are church partnership staff equipped to talk to churches about giving, or can development staff access church partnerships?

DEVELOPMENT AND MOBILIZATION

- Are development and mobilization working in coordination with marketing and communications?

DEVELOPMENT AND FIELD LEADERSHIP

- Does your field leadership appeal for donations for projects from individuals and foundations without coordinating with your development team?

- Does your field leadership provide project details to your development team so they can seek funding and report to donors about progress?

DEVELOPMENT AND FINANCE

- Who creates the messaging for receipts?
- How quickly are donors receipted and thanked?
- Who manages donor issues and needs?
- Is donor data readily available for research or interaction with donors?

DEVELOPMENT AND SENIOR LEADERSHIP

- Do your development team and CEO regularly communicate and coordinate?
- Is your CEO or are your board members available to interact with significant donors?
- Does the senior leadership team provide guidance and direction on what projects to pursue for funding?

The more intentional the conversation is across your teams and the more integrated development is within the organization, the more likely that strategic opportunities will not be missed. Collaboration is essential. Fundraising and development cannot be isolated in your organization. Everyone needs to be a mobilizer of people and resources. Whether your teams engage with new recruits, churches, donors, or foundations, everyone plays a part in helping identify new partnerships that further the mission. Silos reduce unity. Isolation leads to bifurcation which hampers staff collaborating to progress your collective mission.

Fundraising and development cannot be isolated in your organization. Everyone needs to be a mobilizer of people and resources.

Development Audit Key Four: Status of Current Financial Needs

Suppose a person approached your organization today and asked, "If I gave your organization one million dollars, how would you use it?" Are you prepared to answer? In order to answer intelligently, your leadership needs to be regularly updated on financial health and be knowledgeable about potential needs for growth and development. Specific areas of knowledge would include the following:

- General fund status and operational needs
- Staffing needs
- Home office capital needs
- Field projects (by region and type)
- Special projects or things outside of normal operations (i.e., equipment, changes to facilities, new field initiatives)
- Innovation or dreams

Areas with identified needs would strategically benefit from a one- to two-page case statement written in advance. These should be updated on a regular basis so that they are available if an opportunity presents itself. This can be a game changer. Suppose you meet with a donor and plan to ask them to give to one project. In your conversation, they bring up a passion for Asia.

Preparation leads to opportunity.

Because you came with a project already identified in that region that needs funding, you can quickly respond with a relevant ask. Having that information readily available could be the difference between a rejection or the beginning of a new partnership. Preparation leads to opportunity.

Development Audit Key Five: Development Team Role Descriptions and Expectations

Defining who is part of your development team is critical. In small organizations multiple people often contribute to development efforts. Regularly updated role descriptions bring clarity. Whether you are bringing on a new development director or just trying to be more effective in your efforts, this will help each person contribute to their fullest potential with the appropriate expectations. The list below contains the primary roles to define as they relate to fundraising and development:

- Board of directors
- CEO
- Development director
- Major gifts officer
- Donor engagement (receipting, phone calls, thank you)
- Grant writer
- Church relations
- Communications
- Database manager
- Field project manager

Every organization needs to first prioritize leveraging their current team by creating opportunities for the full staff to be part of the solution.

At small to mid-sized organizations, one person may carry many of these responsibilities. Larger organizations may have multiple people in these positions. The key is understanding the realm and responsibilities of each. This is most important as it relates to board members and your CEO. How often will they be available to the development director to meet with donors, travel, or take phone calls on development issues? How much time is your CEO willing to raise funds for your organization?

Are other team members able to provide even limited time to help with development efforts? Most likely in a small to mid-size organization you will not have a multi-member development team. But maybe you have a skilled writer who could give a few hours a week to help write project proposals or grants. Someone skilled with hosting could help run an event. Volunteers could make calls to thank donors. Maybe you have a staff member able to help interface with field leaders to gather project data.

When development is integrated across your organization, your staff will collectively share responsibility for identifying and stewarding donors. Your organization will also be more effective. Smaller organizations often run with an *all-hands-on-deck* mindset. Larger organizations tend to silo and think hiring another person is a solution for everything. But every organization needs to first prioritize leveraging their current team by creating opportunities for the full staff to be part of the solution.

Development Audit Key Six: Culture or Mindset of Fundraising

When it comes to fundraising and development, every organization has a unique culture. Methods, practices, and ideologies coincide with who an organization is. Your CEO, your organization's history, and your board of directors each contribute. Your organization's culture or mindset may have been prayerfully considered, or it may just be a reflection of the way you do things. Your culture needs to be clearly defined and understood and certain parts may need to shift.

Knowledge about your organization's culture is essential for development workers. It saves frustration from taking root. A CEO who understands his or her perspective on fundraising as well as the organization's will help hire a development director who is the best fit for your organization. This helps plans to run smoothly. Here are questions you can use to examine your organization's culture and mindset toward fundraising:

WHO ARE THE DECISION MAKERS?

- Who determines what the organization raises money for – your board, CEO, development director, field leaders?
- Who determines the priority and timing of fundraising projects and campaigns?

WHAT IS YOUR ORGANIZATION'S APPROACH WITH DONORS?

Aggressive

- Conducts face to face meetings after analysis on wealth and giving capacity
- Hosts large events
- Utilizes outside consultants and firms
- Gives very direct requests for funding

Moderate

- Conducts face to face, more relationally based meetings with soft appeals
- Hosts smaller events
- Leans more toward open requests and not direct appeals

WHO MAKES THE FINAL APPEAL TO THE DONOR?

- Your CEO
- A board member
- Your development director
- A major gifts officer

HOW ARE DONATIONS APPROACHED AND ASKED FOR?

Is there a difference between your organization's approach to donors and expectations on missionaries or staff?

To whom does the organization appeal to for donations to the general fund or special projects?

- Foundations
- General fund donors
- Missionary donors

Who can approach donors (foundations or individuals) related to projects and giving?

- Individual staff members
- A development team member
- Your CEO

These questions may be more sensitive than you realize because certain areas or ideas can become unintentionally tightly held. Territory gets set and control gets taken over time without bad intentions. Auditing your development culture enables you to determine if it matches who you want to be or if you have strayed from core organizational values. Grasping this could be the difference between your development director succeeding or never being on the same wavelength with your CEO, ultimately leading to frustration and even dismissal.

Conclusion

A fundraising and development audit is critical to your effort's success. If you are frustrated because your efforts are not producing hoped for fruit, it may be because you did not prepare properly at the beginning.

Growing up in the Midwest working on farms and spending time with farmers, I witnessed the great effort they put into preparation before planting was ever considered. Preparing machinery, the fields, the soil, researching which crops were best in the soil, and understanding the weather were just a few elements that needed their attention. It was only after this that farmers planted the seeds they hoped would provide a bountiful harvest. Randomly going out and throwing seeds of ideas to potential donors provides a limited yield. Most seed will fall on unprepared soil, and your time, energy and effort will be wasted. The diligence of preparation and the discipline of right activities creates the opportunity for your efforts to produce a bountiful harvest that can be stewarded for ongoing ministry effectiveness.

MICHAEL VANHUIS has been with Missio Nexus since September 2015 and currently serves as vice president. He started in missions in 1997 as a Pioneers field missionary in Ghana, West Africa. He's since served in various leadership roles with mission agencies and a large local church. He has a master's of global leadership from Fuller Theological Seminary in Pasadena, California. He and his wife, Laura, have five children and live in Aurora, Illinois.

Chapter Reflections

- When was the last time you conducted a review or audit of your development team and strategies?
- Who are three to five people whom you could gather to begin a development audit?
- What would be a reasonable timeline to complete a full development audit of your organization?

Bibliography and Additional Resources

Panas, Jerold. *Asking: A 59-Minute Guide to Everything Board Members, Volunteers, and Staff Must Know to Secure the Gift.* Emerson & Church Publishers, 2013.

———. *The Fundraising Habits of Supremely Successful Boards: A 59-Minute Guide to Assuring Your Organization's Future.* Emerson & Church Publishers, 2012.

———. *Mega Gifts: Who Gives Them, Who Gets Them.* Emerson & Church Publishers, 2005.

Gravelle, Gilles. *The Age of Global Giving: A Practical Guide for Donors and Funding Recipients of Our Time.*

CHAPTER 6

Beyond Skills and Experience

By Robert Wassel

FOR MONTHS WE INTERVIEWED CANDIDATE AFTER candidate for the director of development role. After each interview I would attempt to convince our executive director and board that each person was "... just not a fit. I can't explain it, but I feel it." Frustration mounted as did the pressure to find someone – anyone. I certainly didn't want to remain in this *interim* development role for ever. That fact alone motivated me to just hire anyone.

I sat across the table from my latest candidate and his wife for an informal restaurant interview. I liked him. Stately, wise and a fundraising veteran, his experience could benefit our organization. His resume demonstrated fundraising success, unlike mine. In fact, his resume was two times longer than mine with exponentially more professional experience. He should have interviewed me!

He answered my complex questions with a contemplative, mature radio voice. He was clear and on cue. I told myself that I just hit the jackpot – the mother lode of fundraisers. He lived in the same state – check. He had the experience we were looking for – check. He could carry a conversation with people from all demographics – check. He was willing to work for what we were willing to pay – check.

And then it happened. In the same breath that he told me his wife would be making "donor visits" alongside him, she reached across the table and ate off my plate. She scooped up a portion of my food and shoved it in her mouth. For most Americans, that is outside the *generally acceptable* category. But, for me, a self-diagnosed ADHD-OCD, that was like stealing a Bible or secretly dating your best friend's girlfriend in high school. You don't do that!

The interview ended with a categorical feeling of "not hired!" What was I going to do? Interview after bad interview, I could not find the right person. Instead, I continued to build the department for ten years and discovered what nonprofits mean by *interim roles*!

The Character Nugget

I grew up in Denver, Colorado, and on the weekends, my mom would take my brother and I to the mountains. Rick would complete his meticulously written journal on the birds he spotted. I would fish and pan for gold. Today, if you held my jar of gold nuggets, you'd only find two. Yet, those two nuggets represent far more than alloy. They are tangible visuals representing irreplaceable memories and hours of meaningful stories.

Everyone needs a few gold nuggets in their jar and that is what the next few pages are about – how to spot the right development director to represent your organization. For the sake of clarity, the development director, as I am defining the role, runs a small to medium development shop that requires her to do almost everything from writing to major donor engagements to board presentations and foundation work. Regardless of the size of your shop, the principles apply broadly.

This jar has two nuggets: a character nugget and an operational nugget. The character nugget is about the person, not the resume. It's about you, your organization, and the connection between both. It is far beyond the scope of personality tests like the *Myers Briggs* or *Enneagram*.

Character is all that matters!
It must form the foundation of
experience and competence.
Without it, a losing battle
ensues that drains your
spirit and motivation.

Suspend your view of competence, forget experience and forget the resume. Character is all that matters! It must form the foundation of experience and competence. Without it, a losing battle ensues that drains your spirit and motivation. So, what is character in this context? The best development director hires have four nonnegotiable character traits: meekness, stewardship, wisdom and integrity.

Meekness

Meekness might be a development director's most critical character trait. As their manager, this quality saves your mental health. Without meekness, supervisors fight a never-ending battle against hubris and pride. A development director once told me that after telling a staff member to do a certain task, this same staff member turned around and did the exact opposite. When asked why he did that, he said, "because my idea was better."

A meek person doesn't judge an idea's worthiness on their own subjective scale before accepting instruction. Rather, a person with meekness keeps a posture of teachability. Meek people approach life as learners, not judgers. Learners listen to gain insights, while judgers listen only for agreement and an opportunity to espouse their opinion.

A person with meekness keeps a posture of teachability.

Imagine being a financial ministry partner sitting across from a not-so-meek fundraiser. Every sentence you speak is either interrupted or abruptly followed by an overwhelming insertion of expert *opinion*. Your thought construction is scrutinized and listened only to gage its fit within their personal worldview. And they essentially know everything, so there is no point in you saying a word. Why would you? You're sitting in the presence of *greatness*! Perhaps you are cringing, but, sadly, this is not hard to imagine.

Furthermore, those with meekness also attain humility when life's difficult trials pass them through the Refiner's fire. This gives birth to genuine and true life as well as humble character. First Peter 4:1–2 says, "... for whoever has suffered in the flesh has ceased from sin, so as to live for the rest of the time in the flesh no longer for human passions but for the will of God" (ESV).

Those who have experienced the sting of pain, loss and suffering have two things going for them. First, they don't argue over pettiness, demanding a stand on paper soapboxes. Life is too short, and they understand and orient themselves toward the higher good – the kingdom of God. Second, they connect with people, deeply, authentically and empathetically.

That relational connectedness is the difference between a person who sees all of life as an exchange of goods and services and a person who understands the higher good often requires losing. Faith-based nonprofits must have development directors who are pastoral listeners and whose personal brokenness allows for real relationships. Ultimately, meek and humble people do not look at relationships as transactions.

A steward refrains from connecting their identity to what they create.

Stewardship

This takes me to the second trait, stewardship. People who culti-vate stewardship live by two non-negotiable postures. First, they recognize that God places others in their lives to steward, not own. Thus, they are non-transactional; they do not see relationships as a means to get something. Because they see how God ordains relationships, they seek to serve other's needs.

Stewards ask, "How, God, do you want me to serve this per-son?" Then they seek ways to discover how to meet that person's needs. Good development directors posture themselves as people who serve and do not take. Stewards forgo asking for funds, implying needs or presenting proposals in lieu of relationship de-velopment; stewards recognize other's needs as the higher good. In doing so, God meets the needs of organizations as he wills, not as organizations may want.

Second, stewards are open-handed with what they produce. Everyone has worked with people who are married to their ideas – its excruciating. In fact, I'd bet you and I have been guilty of that as well. A steward refrains from connecting their identity to what they create. Rather, they connect to the mission of the organization and to others. Development directors who cultivate stewardship are open-handed in their work. They present their ideas not in tightly closed fists but rather in wide open hands. Stewards are spiritually indifferent to anything but God's will. His will, not their identity, guides their actions and postures.

If you don't hire stewards, you hire owners – transactional people who view their own needs as the higher good. Furthermore, their identity will be crushed by any comment they define as less than favorable toward their work. Ownership is not to be confused with responsibility. To say, "take ownership" is to say, "take responsibility." However, development directors who are owners are close-fisted, win-lose people. They must be on top, and they get there by viewing people as a means to an end. This is a common theme in character-deficient development directors.

Stewards are those rare people with whom you leave a conversation feeling like you've just met your next best friend. You feel that way because they listened and genuinely care. Your needs are their concern and your money is completely irrelevant. Development directors who steward financial partners well honor their positions, their organizations, and God.

Wisdom

The third character trait is wisdom. Sounds obvious, right? On the surface, wise directors are well-rounded and well-read on topics from faith to geopolitics to economics and culture. They also engage deeply with virtually anyone, reading macro nuances in a room and sensing micro nuances in people – that's important!

But how many people are truly wise? Do you pray for wisdom, pursue it, or practice it? Proverbs 8:12 says, "I, wisdom, dwell together with prudence; I possess knowledge and discretion" (NIV). Development directors with wisdom know when to speak, what to say, and more importantly, what not to say. I have heard more than enough stories about development directors' speech and behavior that would make anyone embarrassed. Speech that is even remotely borderline, paired with behavior that is not above reproach, will not only ruin individual people, but destroy your organization. Hiring prudent and wise development directors honors God and saves your organization from indescribable trouble.

Friends that run Christian foundations tell me that it is hard to discern between genuine friendship with development direc-

Wise organizational advocates meet others where they are, emotionally, spiritually, and relationally.

tors and façade relationships. They say they sometimes feel like they're being sold a bill of goods as they are told success stories of ministries. Yet, wise development directors represent the organization well by blending full transparency with discretion, a trait that is unfortunately hard to find. They tell the truth even when stories and projects don't go as planned. Wisdom doesn't make excuses, hide truth, or exaggerate successes. That is foolishness motivated by fear.

Furthermore, wise development directors master the art of conversation – asking questions, listening, and engaging in generative dialogue. Wise organizational advocates meet others where they are, emotionally, spiritually, and relationally. They make better decisions, leverage sound judgment and follow the influence of the Holy Spirit with conviction. The higher good drives their motivation, not quotas and pressure to perform. More importantly, James 3:13–15 says that godly wisdom produces deeds done in humility, and earthly *wisdom* produces bitter envy and selfish ambition.

There is a marked difference between self-motivated, *kingdom-minded* development directors and driven, ambitious directors who allow increasing financial targets to influence their mindset and behavior. James 3 continues in verse 17, "The wisdom that comes from heaven is first of all pure; then peace-loving, considerate, submissive, full of mercy and good fruit, impartial and sincere" (NIV). That describes who you want representing your organization! A person with purity does not manipulate others to meet personal goals or organizational targets. Likewise, consideration motivates a person to engage others with deep empathy. And, a person who is impartial does not look at, treat, or even perceive those with wealth as even one percent more important or dignified or desirable than those without means. Seek wise directors!

Integrity

You might assume the trait of integrity goes without saying, especially in a Christian nonprofit setting. However, when discussing the exchange of finances, the topic must be addressed. Integrity has two sides. The obvious side includes not steeling, lying, or manipulating. It aligns your private and public life. The less obvious side refers particularly to consistently applying metrics.

Several years ago, I flew across the country to meet with Zack, a prospective financial partner. As I drove up to his house, I quickly realized that my house could literally fit inside Zack's garage. Of course, he would need to remove the collection of thirteen high-end sports cars so my house would fit!

Admittedly, I was really hoping to drive in one, any of them. My pathetic prayers were answered. It was the Ferrari 458. I'll refrain from boring you with descriptions of the effervescent smell and opulent feel of the leather, the unmistakable sound of the motor, and the peppermint patty feel of the wind blowing through my hair. As we ran the car through its paces, at 25 miles per hour, stopping at every intersection to hydraulically lift the car over the drainage ditch, passed said ditch, stop and hydraulically lower the car down, wash-rinse-repeat at every intersection, I knew I would not be asked, "do you want to drive?"

The restaurant discussion lasted two hours, most of which was me listening to Zack defend why he will not give to missions. He doesn't "want to be complicit in sending missionaries into harm's way." It felt like a verbal beat-down. After returning to the house, Zack dropped me off on the sidewalk. Our time, he decided, had

Taking a posture of learning with others enables them to consider, alongside you, how you might champion kingdom opportunities together.

ended. Watching the Ferrari slowly roll up the gravel driveway, the electronic gate open and close behind him, I glanced to my right to see my super-sub-economy rental car. I looked up to the sky and thought, "Isn't this a sight, the haves and have-nots, separated by a gate."

For days, I was disturbed by that interaction. And then the Lord spoke, "What is the difference between you and him? It's only scale. Just because you buy things that cost less doesn't mean you're any different. If one hundred percent of what you have is mine, why do you treat ninety percent as if it's yours?"

Integrity is not only about ordering your private life to keep it consistent with public life. It's also about ordering your private heart to keep it consistent with your speech and actions. Do I judge myself and my spending habits, as I judge others? Do I apply the metric I happily imposed upon Zack back onto my own habits?

While development directors may spend extraordinary amounts of time studying money in the Bible, they need to graciously and impartially engage others with the Word. Lording that knowledge over others does not persuade them. However, taking a posture of learning with others enables them to consider, alongside you, how you might champion kingdom opportunities together. Just because God gave Zack the ability to make money, does not mean that he is obligated to respond to my need! Seeing people through that lens is a grossly inconsistent application of a metric no one would want imposed upon themselves.

Character Matters

Meekness, stewardship, wisdom, and integrity – do you see those in the people around you? Can you imagine how your organization might function without those character traits? Imagine for a second that your development director is arrogant, close-handed and easily offended, regularly exercises poor discretion and views your financial partners through lenses of partiality and judgment. Not only would that be a disaster for you, it would also ruin your organization.

Like any sin, those traits are not always easy to see. They are subtle, reveal themselves slowly, and often remain hidden until pressure and time constraints mix with the human condition. At that point, you realize you have a serious problem. Don't wait for that to happen. Pursue character development in current directors and character testing in prospective hires to ensure your ministry honors God and people well.

ROB WASSEL is the founder and executive director of *Seeds Global Innovation Lab*, and previously served as the senior vice president of advancement for *Pioneers*. He consults with leaders around innovation, strategy and execution along with biblical stewardship in fundraising. Rob has served nonprofits for more than seventeen years.

Chapter Reflections

- Think about a person you know who forged meek humility in the fire of suffering. What about them is genuine, attractive and inspiring? How can you identify true meekness in others?
- Reflect on a time when your fear of others, ambiguity, or uncertainty produced ownership and control. How could a posture of stewardship have created better results? How can you grow in this area so you can disciple development directors into a stewardship posture?
- Read James 3:17 and create a short list of nonnegotiable beliefs and behaviors that should characterize the lives of development directors. How could these become guiding biblical principles and cultural standards for your organization?
- What unhealthy metrics do you apply to people with wealth but not to yourself? How can you resolve to apply metrics consistently to yourself and others?

Bibliography and Additional Resources

Rodin, R. Scott and Gary G. Hoag. *The Sower: Redefining the Ministry of Raising Kingdom Resources*. ECFAPress, 2010.

CHAPTER 7

To Hire or Not to Hire a Professional Fundraiser

By Keith Sparzak

IN THE EARLY 1800S UNITED STATES President Thomas Jefferson commissioned Meriwether Lewis and William Clark to find a northwest passage from the upper Midwest to the Pacific Ocean. No maps existed for that area, but this did not deter them from departing for their expedition. Starting in Pittsburgh, they traveled up the Missouri River by canoe until they reached the river's headwaters in southwest Montana where they then came face-to-face with the Rocky Mountains.

Continuing their mission required they leave their boats behind to begin an arduous journey over the mountains. Together with their crew, they eventually reached the Pacific, and then three years later made it back home again. They made numerous discoveries along the way, but the journey cost human lives and health. Traveling without a map into unknown territory can be like that.

At a much less impressive level, my wife and I also like to explore unknown territory. I have a confession: we own an old-fashioned road atlas – two actually. Not only do we own them ... *we use them!* In this day of smartphones and GPS studded dashboards, our Rand McNally atlases show wear from frequent use. Google Maps and GPS units are great when you know exactly where you want to go, but what if you don't? What if you are simply exploring?

When we moved to Colorado in 2012, we committed to discover the nooks, crannies, and mountain towns peppered across the western half of our state. Even with a map, we made wrong turns and poor choices – some with significant or potentially serious consequences. Unpaved mountain roads can be unforgiving, but, thankfully, no choices have been fatal – yet!

Much like these examples of exploration, in this chapter, I will explain the journey into the territory of using professionals in fundraising. Others have made their own journeys with various degrees of success or failure in this land. But when *your ministry* considers hiring a development director or contracting a fundraising consultant, it can feel like an expedition into the unknown that can potentially yield great benefits or major, if not disastrous, negative results.

When the Resource Road Runs Out

Your ministry can only grow so far for so long. Eventually, you'll hit a resource dead end where you must consider new ways to raise funds from your existing donor base or secure new donor sources to fuel existing ministry or grow. The road to establishing and sustaining a start-up can be fairly straightforward. Whether by reactive or proactive planning, intuition or even *accident*, a ministry gets established and begins a growth trajectory. If your ministry is successful and maintains its growth, the odds are strong that you will eventually realize the limits of your current resource flow. A change needs to occur to sustain what you attained and/or to expand.

That is when the road essentially runs out. What got you *here* will not get you *there*. What got you *here* is likely the result of your ministry's visionary leader communicating a compelling vision to family, friends, church leaders and a few outside donors who cast their wallets into the support circle. After exhausting his or

What got you *here* will not get you *there*.

her group of existing investors in the vision, your organization is stuck in the *here* until you find a way *there*. Additional complications include donor fatigue or reaching the capacity of standing donors. The vision of your leader, no matter how compelling, only raises a certain amount of funds in a limited seating theater (if you will). The desire and vision to expand are not enough to acquire the means to do it.

Many small and mid-sized ministries also have the following compounding problems:

- Not enough bandwidth to raise resources beyond existing levels.
- Board members with limited or no donor networking capacities.
- Few or no personnel with the essential relational, educational, technical, or strategical skills required to be strong development directors.

This last point is key. Tony Poderis of Raise-Funds.com states:

All non-profit organizations want a development director who has common sense; works hard; prepares to perfection; is courteous, sensitive, and understanding; exudes unbridled enthusiasm; possesses a positive temperament; and is committed to what the organization is doing. And that's just for starters. Let's not forget fundraising knowledge, management experience, superior organizational and communication skills, analytical capabilities, and the ability to conceptualize. Non-profits want all of the above so that their development director will be ready to design, put together, and manage the organization's fundraising campaigns from beginning to end.[1]

Resource Raising Roadblocks

Many dynamics will challenge your efforts to increase funding from outside or unknown sources. The size of any given roadblock varies depending on your organization and the person or group you have assigned to raise resources. You may face difficulties due to skill, psychological or spiritual factors. I mention a few here to illustrate my point:

MOST MINISTRY LEADERS LACK ADEQUATE FUNDRAISING SKILLS. A lot of money is left alongside the road by ministry leaders because they do not know how to read or follow the *development map*. While many raise resources through their passionate ministry promotion, their capacities are usually limited without fundraising training. Those who become effective at raising money have dispositions that fit the part and a desire to learn effective methodologies.

On the other hand, development directors and fundraising consultants come with training and job experience for which most ministry leaders and other organizational personnel have no exposure. This is especially true in reference to strategizing, marketing, networking, social media tactics, donor management systems and software.

FUNDRAISING SHIFTS YOUR LEADER'S FOCUS. When a ministry founder/leader is adept at raising resources, fundraising can become a major distraction. It can keep a leader from advancing the actual ministry because the primary goal shifts to raising money. While

---

1 Tony Poderis, "What's a Good Director of Development Worth?," Raise-Funds, https://www.raise-funds.com/whats-a-good-director-of-development-worth/.

Jesus made money and stewardship an integral part of his teaching, so why do many ministry leaders have such difficulty inviting others to participate in God's work?

the vision and mission remain important, meeting or increasing the budget increases in importance so that more ministry can be done. That subtly or even dramatically shifts the leader's focus from leading vision to raising resources.

ADEQUATE FUNDRAISING REQUIRES SIGNIFICANT RESOURCES. From working networks, to developing and implementing strategies, exploring social media options, corresponding, traveling, writing executive summaries and proposals, following-up and so on, doing fundraising well requires significant human resources and time. Ministry leaders and their teams typically do not have this – at least in ample measure.

INVITING OTHERS TO GIVE CAN BE DIFFICULT. While it is uncomfortable to say it this way, every meeting with a potential donor can become an overt or covert *sales job* designed to reel in another grant. At the same time, most culturally Western people have a strong aversion to asking others for money even when the cause is highly worthy of support. The resulting psychological and emotional challenges for ministry leaders and staff not gifted in and passionate about development work are real and hard to overcome.

Jesus made money and stewardship an integral part of his

teaching, so why do many ministry leaders have such difficulty inviting others to participate in God's work? It likely is not a lack of confidence in the mission, but rather a lack of personal confidence in fundraising. Insecurity or fears of rejection can be directly or indirectly rooted in pride. But regardless of the reason, many leaders and their staff struggle to ask potential donors to partner with their ministries.

A DEEPER SPIRITUAL DIMENSION OFTEN COMES INTO PLAY. Jesus and his followers pose a threat to Satan's temporal terrestrial authority on this earth. Satan actively tries to thwart resources from being raised for mission. He stands opposed to impactful ministry that favors God's purposes and wages war against the *kingdom of light*.

Which Way Should You Turn?

When you reach the end of the road or a major roadblock, your next steps determine your ministry's growth trajectory. Your ministry will have to choose to either maintain current commitments or continue expansion and explore new options to increase finances. If you choose the latter, ministry staff and/or the board will inevitably ask, "Should we think about hiring a development director or fundraising consultant?"

As a member of a few boards, I have participated in several conversations on this topic. Through that experience, I learned to proceed with caution. A wrong turn on the road with regard to hiring or not hiring a development director or fundraising consultant can have significant repercussions especially if your ministry's board is not all in agreement.

Bringing on a professional seems like a logical choice. Fundraising adverse ministry leaders or staff may think:

- "It's finally off of my plate!"
- "She's the professional and will make everything right!"
- "If it works, I'll look like a rock star!"

- "If the funds don't come rolling in, at least it won't be my fault!"

Add whatever other rationale feels right for you.

So ... are you expecting a definitive answer? Here it is: If you and your organization are at a crossroads and think it is time to hire a professional, the answer is a very definite, *MAYBE*! I'm not intentionally trying to be difficult – just honest. Answering this question for your organization requires strong objectivity seasoned with subjectivity and prayer. Your answer will vary depending on your current capacities, existing personnel, financial margins, past history, current ethos, board composition, timing, etc.

Be careful not to miss any road hazard signs or dismiss potential dangers posted along the road which could take you to a precarious point at significant cost. For example, if you casually hire a development director and he or she does not work out, the financial costs are significant. Even if you find an effective one, *it is estimated that the average lifespan of a development director is sixteen to eighteen months*. Let that settle for a moment or two.

When I served in the foundation world, I knew of only a few ministries with development directors that had any significant length of service. The doors typically revolve quickly. In addition, direct and indirect costs for finding a replacement can be as high as $127,650.[2] Direct costs encompass expenses for a development director search, and then the resources invested in the interview process, onboarding, organizational orientation, and so on. Indirect costs include time wasted or lost for a failed hire. Both require significant energy and effort. For *any* organization, this is

---

2 Penelope Burk, "Donor Centered Leadership" (lecture, Association of Fundraising Professionals conference, Vancouver, April 2, 2012), quoted in Raymund Flandez, "The Cost of High Turnover in Fundraising Jobs," *The Chronicle of Philanthropy*, April 2, 2012, https://www.philanthropy.com/article/the-cost-of-high-turnover-in-fundraising-jobs/.

a significant investment (or loss). For smaller ministries, that risk factor is amplified.

Signpost Questions

To help you answer *your* query, I created a list of guiding questions to assist you in making an informed and wise decision. The questions are not exhaustive. As you consider your own context, think of more questions that fit your present challenges. And, let me encourage you to be honest – *brutally honest* – with your answers. So, here is my list:

- Have you conducted a thorough assessment of your current fundraising status and capacities to raise resources from existing funding conduits?
- Have you considered all fundraising options and opportunities available to you as low-hanging fruit that would not require hiring a fundraising professional?
- What process will you employ to come to a point of decision?
- Who should/must be involved in the decision to hire or not hire a professional fundraiser?
- Who could you talk to who would understand your context and who has also wrestled with a decision to hire or not to hire a development director?
- Would working with a fundraising consultant work better for you than hiring a development director?
- Can you afford to hire (or not hire) either a development director or fundraising consultant?
- Have you considered the risks involved and counted the costs of failure?
- Have you considered the potential impacts a professional fundraiser would have on present or acquired donors?
- How will you identify the *right* candidate?
- Are you ready and willing to have your current fundraising methods challenged by a trained fundraising professional?

- Have you prepared an orientation to help a newly hired development director grasp your ministry vision and values so he or she can communicate them with the same passion as your founder or other ministry insiders?
- How will you know when a development director has adopted and conveys your ministry ethos?
- What expectations will you have for a development director?
- How will you define success as it relates to the fruit of the development director's activities, and how will you ensure that your view is in alignment with the development director's view?
- What value are you going to place on relational capacities versus technical skills?

If you determine to hire a development director, great resources on the internet can assist you with searching and interviewing candidates.

Looking Down the Road Ahead

Having been on both sides of the donor–recipient road, I know that a development director can either be a major asset for a ministry's fundraising efforts or an unnecessary, potentially harmful, hindrance. When you find yourself at the intersection where you need to choose between hiring a professional fundraiser or parking where you are at, take time to consider the potential consequences of your decision. Consider the questions presented in this chapter, as well as other questions that apply to your context. Seek outside counsel and dedicate time in prayer before proceeding.

Occasionally taking dicey routes on our Colorado explorations taught me the limitations of maps. Conversely, the map usually leads Suzanne and me well, sometimes leading us on awe-inspiring adventures. Keep that in mind on your fundraising journey. Following the *signs* and asking for directions will help you avoid dangerous and unproductive decisions and guide you to a good place regardless of the direction you turn.

KEITH SPARZAK has served as international director of Community Bible Study since 2016. He oversees the development and implementation of strategies, mission critical activities and assists his team in Colorado Springs to support regional and national Directors, as well as volunteers, in the one hundred twenty countries where CBS has a presence. He previously served for nine years with a Christian foundation as a program officer, and twenty years in a variety of pastoral positions: global outreach, as well as associate and lead roles.

Chapter Reflections

- How would you and your team define your ministry's fundraising culture at the board and staff levels?
- Summarize your fundraising strategy in tangible terms. If you do not have a clear strategy, how will you begin to refine or create one, and who should you include in the process?
- What ministries are like yours both in focus and scale? Create a list and arrange conversations with each to learn more about how they've overcome their fundraising challenges and benefited from opportunities.
- Are you determined to move forward with a fundraising consultant or development director? Before you finalize your decision, ensure that you've met with a variety of organizations to learn more about how they've done approached this.

Bibliography and Additional Resources

Aly Sterling Philanthropy. "How to Write a Development Director Job Description: 4 Key Tips." Last updated September 30, 2017, https://alysterling.com/development-director-job-description/. While this is not a faith-based source, it has good guidelines.

Andringa, Robert. "What Is the Board's Role in Fundraising?" ECFA, https://www.ecfa.org/Content/What-Is-the-Boards-Role-in-Fundraising-NP. A good basic article on this subject.

Reis, Jeremy. "25 Interview Questions to Hire Your Development Director." Nonprofit Donor, https://nonprofitdonor.com/25-interview-questions-to-hire-your-development-director/. This article offers a solid list of interview questions.

CHAPTER 8

Biblical Fundraising 101

By Barbara Shantz

CALLING A FUNDRAISING PROFESSIONAL FOR ADVICE can be a fearful exercise. But doing fundraising on your own might be even more frightening. Take heart – your calling or ministry opportunity can be funded. This chapter will give you ideas about how to start your fundraising efforts on a biblical foundation.

Get Ready for War

I was on my way to teach at a fundraising conference when I met *Anika*[1] on the bus to the conference center. She turned to me and said, "I can't believe that I'm supposed to take a week off ministry to go to a fundraising seminar. I have so much to do. They want me to raise my own salary AND raise funds for the ministry from among the people where I work. The people in my area are poor. We can't ask *them* for money!"

Later over dinner with several participants, *Nathan* confided that he was attending the seminar to find out enough about fundraising to start a business. He excitedly told us his plan which ended with a triumphant, "So then the business will pay

---

1 Names throughout this chapter have been changed to retain privacy.

for the ministry, and we won't have to worry about fundraising after that!"

I asked, "Do you have past business experience?" He shrugged his shoulders. I grinned mischievously and said, "What if starting a business is way harder than fundraising?" He looked at me dubiously but grinned back.

On the way to my room after dinner I met a young woman named *Beth*. She had just taken a part-time job as an organization's first fundraiser. She smiled as she told me about her fundraising experience. She was well-qualified to take them where they wanted to go financially, but they wanted her to use biblical methods. She didn't know what that meant.

The war was on. This war is against the mental block that stops the spread of the gospel[2] – the place (and fear) of money in ministry. But this war is not hopeless; it is fought with the prayers of God's people:

> "For we do not wrestle against flesh and blood, but against the rulers, against the authorities, against the cosmic powers over this present darkness, against the spiritual forces of everlasting in the heavenly places. Therefore, take up the whole armor of God, that you may be able to withstand in the evil day, and having done all, to stand firm." (Ephesians 6:12–13, ESV)

Is it extreme to compare fundraising dislikes to a war? Not at all. Funding your ministry is just not that complicated. Satan blinds us and, in many cases, convinces us that doing ministry is easier than funding it. But the opposite is true. God gives us fundraising as a blessing. It is a quest for God's presence in ministry

---

2 The Lausanne Movement has identified Ministry Fundraising as a barrier to the global completion of the Great Commission. The issue group, the Lausanne Ministry Fundraising Network, gives free 7-week courses as an introduction to biblical fundraising, http://www.ministryfundraisingnetwork.org/.

God shows up when we recognize the FULL mission of God – which includes the funding of our ministries.

and a skill to be honored. Without that belief, pressure mounts as days go by, and it becomes dark. This eventually destroys leaders and their joy in God's plans.

My favorite part in teaching fundraising seminars is where God shows up. Once ten or twenty scriptures have been studied, God pierces through the fear and disbelief to what Henri Nouwen referred to as a "conversion" – seeing money through "a divine eye, a divine ear, a divine heart."[3] God shows up when we recognize the FULL mission of God – which includes the funding of our ministries.

Here are a few reasons why God might want you to fundraise:

- If you could do the job alone, the ministry would be yours, not that of the Church and certainly not that of God.
- You accomplish teamwork and acquire new emotional skills when you include those who give as part of your ministry community.
- Every giver gains deep dignity and joy when giving.
- Your faith builds when you see God's *hobby* of supplying his people and funding from places you least expect, giving you fresh vision.

As Henri Nouen says, "Fundraising is first and foremost a form

---

3 Henri J. M. Nouwen, *A Spirituality of Fundraising* (Nashville, TN: Upper Room Books, 2011), 19.

of ministry. It is as spiritual as giving a sermon, entering a time of prayer, visiting the sick or feeding the hungry!"[4]

Christians often separate their faith from their finances. To complicate matters, distrust increases because what a fundraiser does hides behind words like *development* or *advancement*. If you don't like the word *fundraising* due to its historic negative connotations, consider *charitable giving* to keep the intended goal clear: relationships meant to steward generous giving.

The global church takes Christ to the nations as a team. We handle ministry together under God's leadership. All of us – including those who give – work collectively towards the vision statement of the Bride of Christ – the great multitude from all peoples and languages worshiping Jesus (Revelation 7:9–12).

Can You Say, "FUNDRAISING?"

It starts at the top. Most are familiar with the idea of board members fundraising for, or at least giving to, a ministry. Sadly, however, funding organizational growth is not yet part of mandatory coursework in seminaries and Christian institutions preparing people for ministry. Most graduates enter their new work blissfully unaware. After crossing the threshold of their *godly assignment*, they discover the key to the miraculous drawer of cash for operating the work is missing. They can't skim over the topic either. They find out that money is not "evil mammon" but what enables ministry. As Joel Carpenter famously said, "More money means more ministry."[5]

---

4 Nouwen and Mogabgab, *Spirituality of Fundraising*, vii.

5 Larry Eskridge and Mark A. Noll, eds., *More Money, More Ministry: Money and Evangelicals in Recent North American History* (Grand Rapids, MI: Eerdmans, 2000), 401.

According to Carver's Policy Governance® model,[6] an organization's direction – *the end* – is set by the board and strategy for accomplishing that end – *the means* – is set by leadership. Those who struggle through the ministry's strategy and decisions are the best fundraisers for the organization. However, as the ministry grows, they can no longer maintain the number of relationships needed to sustain the work. That's when you need to hire a fundraiser.

Nathan, who I met at the seminar welcome dinner, was "absolutely thrilled" to be heading up a new ministry. It fit his calling, and he knew he was the right person for the job. When his board sent him to the fundraising seminar to look at the biblical basis of money, he was intrigued. But he was sure that it would be better to avoid fundraising altogether by starting a business to cover the costs.

On the second day of our seminar, I assured Nathan that we would look at funding ministry out of business. Sometimes it works, but not usually when led by a ministry person. It is a deep topic that the BAM (Business as Mission)[7] movement has thoroughly researched.

The next day Nathan told me that the Lord spoke to him about pride in his heart – the pride of not wanting to ask others for money. Wow. God showed up. Never before had a student so readily admitted that to me. Nathan's sensitivity to the Holy Spirit blessed me. I learned from it.

Nathan's hesitancy is common. *The ask* often scares people away from fundraising. But that segment of the giving process is actually only a small part of the annual cadence of a relationship

---

6 "Home," Policy Governance, accessed June 18, 2020,

http://www.policygovernance.com/.

7 Norah Hughes, "Mission Agencies: Challenges and Opportunities for Business as Mission," *Business as Mission Think Tank* (2015), eds. Jo Plummer and Mats Tunehag, https://www.bamglobal.org/wp-content/uploads/2015/11/BMTT-IG-BAM-Mission-Agencies-Final-Report-November-2015.pdf.

with a donor. Relationships with each giver are even more unique than your ministry. Estimates vary, but here is what the annual time with a giver could look like:

First Year

RESEARCH – 30%. When a potential giver is put forward, about 25% of your time during the first year will be exploring that donor's interest and educating them about your ministry.

FRIENDSHIP – 40%. In the years thereafter, likely around 40% of your annual time with a giver will be for developing your professional friendship as you journey together in life and ministry.

THE ASK: 10%. As you begin to understand the giver, *the ask* might still be uncomfortable, but it is simply part of an informed relationship that is sometimes even initiated by the giver! Therefore, I estimate less than ten percent of your annual time with a giver will actually be *asking* for a donation depending on how frequently they give.

THANKS AND REPORTS: 20%–50%. Givers should be thanked and appreciated for their donations with honest and detailed reports that level parallel to their giving. At least twenty percent of the first year should be spent giving reports and receiving feedback on the giver's satisfaction with the use of their donation.

While it is not up to donors to determine ministry vision or strategy, it is important to receive input from them. We are not above reproach or taking suggestions from others who put their heart and treasure into partnership.

If this is not the current culture of your ministry, read and study on. How did Jesus and his disciples raise funds for their ministry? The search to find fundraising parallels for church and other ministries in the Bible can be a great team-builder for staff and volunteers.

Have You Utilized the Gifts of a Salesperson?

Now that Nathan had accepted the idea of fundraising, he was like a sponge ready to soak up information. Should he raise funds for his salary or for the ministry? Anika and Nathan began to work on their now similar situations.

As the sole employee of a ministry, it would probably be more sustainable for Nathan to raise funds for the organizational vision rather than for his own salary. It usually takes a different type of person to start something than to maintain it, so this way the ministry could continue even if the Lord sent Nathan elsewhere. In this case, Nathan's salary would be part of ministry costs.

For Anika, I suggested she raise funds for her salary. She could tap into gifts from family and friends. Then, as she disciples new believers in the poorer neighborhood where she serves, she could teach them to be givers to God, using Paul's "fundraising book," Philippians, as her textbook.

Even though the church in Philippi was young (about a decade old), small, persecuted, and poor, Paul lifted up the congregation as a model of giving. There is no mention that the Philippians received funding from a mother church as a church plant. Followers of Jesus in Philippi, apparently, financially sustained their own work, regularly gave to Paul as their missionary, *and* gave a generous offering to fundraiser Paul for the church in Jerusalem! This book provides an excellent team study in fundraising procedures with something relevant for every fundraising team member!

As you focus on Philippians, you can see that *every* believer is called to *go* and make disciples – no matter where they are or what their occupation; and *every* believer is called to *give*. You don't need to decide for others how they should help or how much they should give. This is between the believer and their Lord. Your responsibility is to present the opportunities to everyone. In fact, I have found that God *loves* to turn our *sure* plans and ideas upside down. It's best to work on your plans and then laugh with delight with God when you see him change them for the better.

You don't need to decide for others how they should help or how much they should give. This is between the believer and their Lord. Your responsibility is to present the opportunities to everyone.

The most overlooked workforce for fundraising advice and networks might be salespeople. Imagine if Anika knew a committed Christian car salesperson who could *sell* her calling in her home town. A salesperson could set up meetings where Anika could talk about her work and help her fundraise for her salary. This would not be to do it *for* her but to give suggestions on marketing. This person could also open up their sales network to host events for her.

Imagine if a real estate salesperson was Nathan's advisor on how to find contacts for his ministry. Real estate professionals are highly disciplined in discretion and trained in reading a person's character. Such an advisor could help Nathan learn which people might be most interested in joining his volunteer and giving teams.

Financial advisors can help followers of Jesus steward their charitable funding. Christian ministries need to partner with financial advisors so they can inform their clients about your important ministry. God does not supply us with money to get more but to steward what we have so that we can give more. [8]

---

8 In 2007 it became possible to become a certified, "Kingdom Advisor" – a trained financial planner who utilizes biblical principles of stewardship. For more information go to https://kingdomadvisors.com/.

Business is not the same as ministry, but there are certainly transferable concepts. If you are not sure if you can afford a fundraiser, build relationships with all the salespeople you can and get their input on how to raise funds. Salespeople love to help in ministry and are often overlooked because they are not always wealthy. Their self-starting skills and training to be bold to *ask* for a sale will be a treasure to you. Like donors, sales people should not be allowed to take over the vision. However, give them space to speak their mind; their good ideas will be a gift to help you refine your ministry.

Concepts That Lead to Success

Business guru Peter Drucker once said, "Culture eats strategy for lunch." In Christian nonprofits, a biblical fundraising culture is imperative. Every team member needs to know how to explain why they work or volunteer with an organization in their own, honest way. They are walking billboards for your ministry and should be able to recognize the signs of a potential volunteer or donor. Furthermore, team members who participate in fundraising should be celebrated. Their job satisfaction draws others into giving.

Remember Beth, the fundraiser attending the week-long seminar? There are not many, if any, who grow up thinking, "Someday, I want to be a fundraiser!" So, when you find someone who enjoys connecting generous givers to your important ministry projects, encourage them in their biblical fundraising! They are an honored group who God has especially called to take your givers on the journey of stewarding *all* that he has given.

Following are basics that will help you and your fundraiser(s) develop a biblical fundraising culture:

POSITION PROFESSIONAL FUNDRAISERS APPROPRIATELY. A professional fundraiser serves to accelerate leadership fundraising capabilities by setting up communication opportunities with donors. Do

NOT fall into the trap of asking your fundraiser – who capably fundraises for projects – to set the strategy for the ministry. Leaders are charged with God's *vision*. They set the guardrails.

COOPERATE WITH AND ENCOURAGE YOUR FUNDRAISER. A Christian fundraiser will lean on the Holy Spirit's urging to present the right project at the right time to the right funder. Resist the temptation to put the entire responsibility of the budget on the shoulders of your fundraiser. There are often additional ways to bring revenue into an organization.

A skilled fundraiser will track their activities rather than raised funds because activities will eventually produce funding. When it comes to people, there are no shortcuts and no certain predictions. No one can be sure of what a donor will give. Trying to coerce a competent fundraiser into forcing a donation from their relationships will leave you with fewer donors and eventually, no fundraiser.

CREATE A CULTURE WHICH CELEBRATES FUNDRAISING AND GIVING PARTICIPATION. Invest in on-boarding volunteers and staff which includes training to develop each person's generous giving comprehension, including an *elevator pitch* – a memorized, 30-second explanation of how their work positively affects the outcome of the organization.

RESOURCE AND PARTICIPATE IN YOUR FUNDRAISING STRATEGY. Resources + activities = outputs, outcomes, and impact. Your fundraiser will need your encouragement and participation in all of the following at minimum:

- Providing internal processes that make giving *easy* – especially for online giving.
- Partnering with professionals in marketing and communications to produce brochures, proposals and reports to enhance your engagement with givers. The quality and frequency of

communications will directly correlate to your productivity and success in fundraising.

- Securing good equipment including a laptop computer, mobile phone and printer.
- Developing a reasonable travel and hospitality budget to meet new donors and thank current donors. Fundraisers need long-term relationships with givers for their gifts to continue. Understand that the ROI from traveling a distance and taking a potential donor out for dinner might not show up until next year's budget, later or not at all.
- Producing trustworthy accounting and accurate year-end financial reports. Do NOT expect a fundraiser to stretch the truth to get funding. If a funded project fails, report that immediately. Do NOT cover it up.
- Fostering a fundraising culture where current donors, staff and volunteers invite their networks to events where a fundraiser can speak to them. (Important: if your staff or volunteers generally do not give to the ministry, it's usually a good idea to find out why. There may be internal issues that need to be exposed.)

This short chapter only scratches the surface of how God will lead you in the ministry of fundraising. Whether you're raising money for ministry like Nathan, salary *and* ministry funds like Anika or simply supporting a willing fundraiser like Beth, pray, trust, and let God choose your funders. Watch for his opportunities!

BARBARA SHANTZ has advised hundreds of nonprofit organizations from more than fifty countries in fundraising. She wrote this article when she operated her own business, Give Way Visioneering. In 2019, Barbara joined the staff of The Gideons International in Canada | ShareWord Global. She lives with her husband, Steve, in New Brunswick, Canada, near their children and grandchildren.

Chapter Reflections

- What are three of the most generous things people have done for you?
- What two generous giving stories from your own life give you joy and satisfaction?
- What misconceptions do you recognize you have had about the word, "fundraising?"
- If you are hesitant to engage in fundraising, what specifically bothers you about it? Do a word search on it in the Bible and then take your concerns to the Lord in prayer for his response.

Bibliography and Additional Resources

Doolittle, Cameron. *Joy Giving: Practical Wisdom from the First Christians and the Global Church*. Rophe House, 2018.

CHAPTER 9

Mindsets and Postures

By Robert Wassel

I JOINED THE NAVY AT AGE seventeen and ended up on the aircraft carrier USS *Nimitz*. One night as I prepared for *flight deck duty*, I was told that I would be the only person on the flight deck from midnight to 4:00 a.m. This was not just any night cruising the Mediterranean by moonlight. We traveled through the single roughest storm of our six-month deployment. We skirted around the Falkland Islands, just before Cape Horn, in 26-foot seas. The wind across the deck gusted upwards of 70 mph!

They strapped me into a harness and used a carabiner to secure me to a rope that laced inside the tie-down points on the deck. Armed with, would you believe it, a flashlight, pen, and paper, I made my rounds across the back of the flight deck to log the status of a handful of aircraft that could not fit inside the hanger bay. I recorded whether they had blown off the deck and checked that they were tightly secured. Why wait until morning? Only in the Navy.

I would take a few steps, unhook the carabiner from one rope and secure it to another, take a few steps, and then repeat the process. Just so I could say I did it, I made my way to the back port (right) side of the carrier, secured the carabiner onto the last tie-down point, and leaned out over the water as far as I could, at about forty-five degrees, all while being held up by the rope. There was a powerful light mid-way down the ship, flooding the water. I distinctly remember watching the water rise and fall, as the 1,092-foot ship was getting tossed in the sea like a john boat. Exhilarating! This was an opportunity for adventure!

A childhood spent in the mountains experiencing outings almost every weekend embedded this mindset inside my DNA and prepared me for my Navy experiences. It flows out of me with little effort. Mindsets and postures are the orientation each person has toward work and others, and they work in sync. As I think, I orient. For example, I operate with a behavior, or posture, that demonstrates an adventure mindset.

While character is the primary indicator of a development director's ability to serve an organization well, four operational mindsets and postures ensure job success: scientist, motivator, connector and visionary. I will explain why these are so important for the remainder of this chapter.

The Scientist

The mindset of a scientist is potentially the hardest to develop, yet critically important. When faced with a challenge or problem, people tend to think *convergently* gathering facts, reducing information and *converging* down to a solution. However, scientists are *divergent* thinkers. They don't rush to *converge*, but comfortably operate within ambiguity and uncertainty. They know the greatest insights will be gained inside spaces of *divergence.*

Divergent thinking opens our minds to unimaginable possibilities freeing us from premature judgments. *Divergent* thinkers are curious and desire to make better and more insightful decisions. When you apply that mindset to a development director, what might the posture look like?

As the founder of Seeds Global Innovation Lab, I do a lot of experimentation – we call it *testing prototypes*. A prototype is simply a rough representation of an idea, and testing prototypes

Divergent thinking opens our minds to unimaginable possibilities freeing us from premature judgments.

is the second critical element in experimentation. A development director must be willing and comfortable thinking *divergently*, and then she needs to orient her behavior by not perpetuating archaic methods.

Sure, there may be tried and true fundraising methods, but experimentation is about co-creating new solutions and connecting with those you serve. It forces you to question your assumptions about your constituents and build out novel solutions that add value, both to the organization and to end-users. To master a mindset and posture of experimentation, you need to believe your assumptions about who you serve are probably incorrect (mindset), seek deep insights about their values and beliefs, create prototypes to test with them, and then repeat that process continually (posture).

I recently heard a story about a development director who was convinced he had a brilliant fundraising idea. After sharing this idea with his team, they asked him how he would gain insights from donors to better understand their values and build prototypes to test with those donors. Instead of creating and executing presumptuous and expensive campaigns that could fail and perpetuate outdated paradigms, his team encouraged rapid prototyping as a means to gain confidence in the effectiveness of the idea. Experimenting, quickly and with feedback loops from your end-users, is a reliable way to mitigate expensive campaigns all while adding value to those we serve.

The Motivator

The second mindset is motivator. Try to avoid visions of Chris Farley, the motivational speaker! When I think of motivation, I don't see it as synonymous with *driven*. In fact, a mentor challenged me saying, "Do you really think we should hire people who are *driven*? Was Jesus *driven*?"

I believe we've created a false positive around that word as if Jesus was calling us to *drive* ministry, *drive* people, *drive* campaigns, *drive* funding and *drive* expansion. Where are we *driving* them – into the ground, over a cliff, across the country? *Driven* connotes the car operates continually in the red zone, at 6,000 RPM's or higher. It runs over others because the higher good is accomplishment, production, and objectives. It fails to stop, think, contemplate, and reorient.

Jesus says we need to *die*, not *drive*. Instead of being *driven*, motivation connotes something internal that fuels your posture. And, when it is specifically applied to yourself, as in *self-motivated*, motivation takes on a very different feel than being *driven*.

When I was the senior vice president of advancement, I would tell new hires, "We have a CRM called *Serenic*. Here are five names of people who know it well. Connect with them and have an eighty percent mastery of the system within the next eight weeks." I would provide them with a broad framework of our context, their job description and our philosophy, but execution was up to their self-motivation.

I hired self-motivated people that did not need hand-over-hand guidance. They only needed an initial point in the right direction. The rest was up to them. They were self-motivated to learn, try and fail. A few did not begin with fundraising competency, but I mentored and coached them where I sensed gaps needed filling.

Interestingly, the mindsets of motivators and scientists cannot be decoupled. When you maintain an experimentation posture, you fail frequently; that's the reason why you experiment. When an engineer builds a bridge prototype in a lab, his goal is not to prove to everyone how beautiful it is. Instead, his goal is to stress test it with weight, break it, learn about weak points, and then do that again to make the bridge stronger. When you build prototypes to test with those you serve, your goal is to question assumptions, gain insights on what matters to them, and then repeat the process again to break old, failed strategies and discover new ones.

Now, imagine how difficult this is for a person without self-motivation. He loses energy, becomes discouraged, and seeks quick *wins* over longer lasting success. Furthermore, if organization leaders don't understand the value of rapid prototyping and the benefits of failure, they won't allow motivators to experiment. Tying your identity too tightly to the image of the organization is a character issue with which anyone can struggle.

Equally important, if your organization fails to celebrate wins and hard sacrifices because of incorrectly believing appreciating staff steals glory from God, your organization will never adopt a posture of failing forward through experimentation. If there is one absolute truth about motivators, it's this: they won't tie themselves to organizations that fail to celebrate staff for their passionate and sacrificial investment into an organization. Almost every leader I speak with publicly argues that their organization celebrates its people. But almost every staff member I speak with privately argues the opposite.

Acts 14:27 says that Paul and Barnabas returned to Antioch and "reported all that God had done through them ..." (NIV). And, I recall Jesus saying that the woman who poured expensive perfume on his head would be remembered throughout history (Matthew 26:12–13). Don't be afraid to appreciate people, foster a culture of celebration and recognize failing (forward) as a huge step toward insights for future success.

The Connector

Malcolm Gladwell, in his book *The Tipping Point*, refers to three types of people: connectors, mavens, and salesmen (I prefer to call them *closers*). At the risk of butchering his meaning, I'll refrain from exhaustive exposition. On a basic level, mavens are industry experts, closers can close deals, and connectors construct bridges between people and resources. A mindset of a connector is paramount in the development space, and, I'd argue, it comes from a little of both nature and nurture.

I'm a natural connector. I think it and do it without any thought. My successes are rooted in uncountable experiences with friends and strangers who bridged relational gaps for me time and time again. Every job I've had – and I've had many – came about because of a connector used by God to join my passion with an opportunity. Even when I lacked passion and was driven out of need, connectors have been invaluable to me.

Think for a second, who built bridges on your behalf and pointed you toward others? Perhaps you've been a connector, helping someone get a job, get resourced or get help. When your victories and success rest on connectors, you deeply value that posture and orient yourself to do the same.

Development directors must be connectors! Although they need to speak professionally about campaigns, initiatives or projects, they also need to be people who work in partnership with mavens. These industry experts often oversee or run the projects for which you are fundraising.

Frank was a maven I worked closely with. Frank ran a huge, global project that received more than one million dollars in funding. While Frank started the project with a few other people, he was the US-based catalyst behind it. He'd travel overseas six times each year implementing, evaluating, and coaching around that project. I learned a lot from Frank, so much so that I'm very well versed in the project research, white-papers, language, philosophy, rationale, strategy, execution, and outcomes.

Yet even though there were times when I was the sole organizational advocate and communicator in a meeting, I'm not the maven. If your shop is small, and you operate as the owner operator, you'll need to temporarily step into maven space, but that is not the development director's primary role.

One of the greatest highlights for our ministry partners was when they could meet or travel overseas with Frank, the maven. No replacement exists for that. No knowledge I gain or espouse can replace that for a partner.

The mindset and posture of connector is a necessary and beneficial trait for a development director and the development department. Posturing yourself this way creates a structure to better meet the needs of those you serve. Development directors need to think it and breathe it. Connectors introduce people, bridge gaps and make relationships happen, but they need to refrain from posturing as the hero of the story. To do that, they must refrain from seeking the primary position and posture themselves as second.

The Visionary

The final mindset for a development director is that of a visionary. Vision guides development directors to orient themselves properly.

Each organization maintains a historical narrative, the story of its founder and how it came to be. That story is extremely critical to the vision of the organization. It holds exciting victories alongside painful memories. And, as a faith-based nonprofit, that story is woven into the meta-narrative of the gospel. It connects emotionally with how God brought together people to serve and sacrifice in your organization in fulfillment of a part of his mission. It connects with burdens God placed in your hearts and causes others to want to be a part of your organization's story and God's story.

But sometimes passion and motivation drive too much, and the historical narrative of an organization subverts its position with the meta-narrative of the gospel. Instead of orienting your organizations as subservient to the gospel, you elevate your own story. Brand worship among ministries is a far too prevalent and ugly form of idolatry.

Visionaries are moved, impassioned, and burdened to sacrifice. As such, they connect with partners on a supernatural level not constructed by human emotion.

This misalignment can cause fear, pressure, and uncertainty. You may make poor decisions in order to preserve your organizational narrative. Development directors who don't balance the organizational vision appropriately can easily posture themselves to manipulate, exaggerate, push, and overreach in their quest to raise funds. If you make the meta-narrative subservient to your organization's narrative, you operate out of a preservation mindset *driven* by the human condition

Conversely, visionaries can hold the organization's narrative as a steward, passionate about how it came to be and what God is doing but orienting it correctly under the meta-narrative. In one sense, organizations are servants of a higher narrative, and development directors need to posture appropriately. That is the mark of a true visionary. Without a God-given, deeply buried burden to realize the vision of the organization, these mindsets and postures are perfunctory, at best, and development directors become only parrots of information.

Those you hire must be sincerely moved by the mission, vision and story of your organization. If there is little evidence of earnest connectedness, paired with a burden to "do something about it," your candidate will serve better elsewhere. Visionaries are moved, impassioned, and burdened to sacrifice. As such, they connect with partners on a supernatural level not constructed by human emotion. You want visionaries representing your organization!

Why Mindsets and Postures Matter

Scientist, motivator, connector and visionary are four operational mindsets that increase the effectiveness of your development director. These also enhance a development department and improve the overall internal health of your organization.

Imagine a development director and department devoid of those traits. Without a scientist mindset, a development director operates out of assumptions and old fundraising models. He does not listen to constituents, and his decisions are rooted in limited perspectives, building linear strategies that lose their strength over time. Without a motivator mindset, your organization leader needs to step in to manage and direct the majority of day-to-day development operations, wasting precious time and energy thinking for others.

When your development department lacks a leader with a connector mindset, it becomes run by a person who insists, even privately, on being the hero of every story. Rather than building appropriate bridges to benefit ministry partners, this leader unsuitably place herself in the position of a maven, the expert on all things. And, a development director who lacks vision fails to communicate out of empathy and passion. Rather, he or she comes across as someone doing nothing more than filling a vacancy until moving on to something better.

By cultivating these natural and learned mindsets and postures, development directors ensure the success of their teams and fulfill their spiritual roles which serve the higher good. When they see their primary role as *kingdom* ambassadors, that becomes the main filter through which all of their mindsets and postures are expressed. So, whether you have the natural mindset of an adventurer or are developing the postures and mindsets of a scientist, motivator, connector or visionary, keep in mind that your gifts and efforts to grow enable you to serve God's *kingdom* effectively.

ROB WASSEL is the founder and executive director of Seeds Global Innovation Lab, and previously served as the senior vice president of advancement for *Pioneers*. He consults with leaders around innovation, strategy and execution along with biblical stewardship in fundraising. Rob has served nonprofits for more than seventeen years.

Chapter Reflections

- Divergent thinking is a key aspect of the scientist mindset. What are your cognitive barriers to thinking divergently? What causes your greatest discomfort with ambiguity or uncertainty? Do you feel tempted to jump to solutions? Do you fear the *wrong idea* might get too much attention?
- Hiring motivators as development directors is paramount. How will you determine if a person you're considering to be your development director is self-motivated, or conversely, overly dependent?
- As you consider Malcomb Gladwell's three types of people – mavens, connectors and closers – how will you help position your development director to take a leading role in connecting? What expectations do you have about their participation in other roles (maven and closer)?
- What place does your organization's narrative hold in relationship to the gospel meta-narrative? Are you willing to let systems, models, or even your *brand* die for the sake of God's kingdom? How will you talk to your visionary development director about this?

Bibliography and Additional Resources

Hoag, Gary G., R. Scott Rodi, and Wesley K. Willmer. *The Choice: The Christ-Centered Pursuit of Kingdom Outcomes*. ECFAPress, 2014.

CHAPTER 10

The Proverbs 16:9 Approach

By Chris Winkler

IN HIS BOOK, *A SPIRITUALITY OF FUNDRAISING*, Henri Nouwen says, "From the perspective of the gospel, fundraising is not a response to a crisis. Fundraising is, first and foremost, a form of ministry."[1]

Whether it is a direct mail campaign, a gift-in-kind opportunity, a one-on-one meeting with a major donor, or some other fund development activity, raising funds in a godly way is *ministry*. Those who give are true partners in the work of global mission, and fund development professionals have the special opportunity to serve and minister to their partners in a significant way.

The purpose of this chapter is to help mission organization fund development professionals understand who their donors are and discover how to best minister to them using file analysis and moves management.

Donor File Analysis

Ministry to donors is an important part of a mission organization's overall ministry regardless of donation size, frequency or

---

1 Henri J. M. Nouwen, *A Spirituality of Fundraising* (Nashville, TN: Upper Room Books, 2011), 16.

type. However, not all donors carry the same expectations when they make a gift. Some play a more integral role in organizational function than others. The organization also has a responsibility to steward its limited resources – including staff, time and money – in a way that honors God and ministers to donors where they are in their spiritual journey and their connection to the organization.

With this in mind, it is important to gain an appropriate understanding of the donor file to the organization. Ministry to donors is more easily done through file segmentation, but if you don't know what is in that file, creating a plan becomes more challenging and might be futile. Consider the following when conducting an analysis:

WHAT PERCENTAGE OF REVENUE COMES FROM WHAT PERCENTAGE OF THE DONOR FILE? For instance, in many organizations 90% of revenue comes from 10% of the donor base, or 80% of revenue from 20% of donors. Answering this question helps the development team determine reliance on certain donors and if there are segments (e.g. major donors, mid-level donors[2], etc.) that should be expanded.

WHAT PERCENTAGE OF DONORS GIVE REGULARLY? Compare your numbers of regular and sporadic donors. Analyze the gift intervals of regular donors: annual, quarterly, monthly. For monthly givers, see if their gift is set up automatically or done manually by mail, phone or online. This helps the development team consider when or how to establish a special monthly giving program, what focus to give to a year-end giving campaign, and the importance of follow-up with pre-lapsed and lapsed donors.

---

2 For the purposes of this chapter, I am using common industry definitions of these segments. Major donors give more than $10,000 in cumulative gifts annually, and mid-level donors cumulatively give between $1,000 and $10,000 each year.

WHERE ARE DONORS LOCATED? Concentrations of donors can make regional events or placement of a staff person in an area a viable option for future development work. Factor in revenue to this analysis to find out whether you have a concentration of mass-level donors or major donors in a particular area. A small number of major donors in an area could represent a far greater percentage of revenue than a large cluster of mass-level donors.

WHAT ARE DONORS' INTERESTS? Some donors may only give to appeals of a certain type or centered in a particular geographic region. The way a donor is acquired gives clues about how they want to be ministered to. For example, a donor who makes a memorial gift might appreciate a follow-up touch around the one-year anniversary of that first gift, or someone acquired through a digital strategy may prefer digital communication[3].

THROUGH WHAT CHANNELS ARE DONORS ENGAGING WITH YOUR ORGANIZATION? Are most donors still mailing in checks? What is the balance between online and offline giving? Do a high percentage of email recipients make a gift? Building off of strengths and filling in weaknesses through this analysis helps identify better ways to reach donors and increase revenue.

While not comprehensive, this overview is designed to help you start your donor analysis. The rest of this chapter looks at how to use this analysis to minister effectively to the various donor file segments.

---

3 While this is usually true, it is not always the case. Typically, multi-channel cultivation is the best default strategy to take if preference is not known.

Methods for Planning Donor Engagement

Two extremes tend to dominate the professional approach to working with donors in the Christian fund development world. Thankfully, a third option offers a more appropriate and effective approach for mission organizations.

The "Spirit" Approach

Fund development professionals on the extreme of the "Spirit" approach argue that because God is sovereign, we should just show up and "let the Spirit move." They may say, "The donor is going to give whatever God lays on their heart, so I will just go and report back to the donor on their last gift, then pray with them. If they choose to give, then great! If not, it is the Lord's will." In this paradigm, fund development professionals are passive participants.

However, few would consider exclusively taking this approach when serving people groups, translating Scripture or preaching the gospel. This approach ignores tools the Lord provides to increase effectiveness. For those who minister to donors, planning calendars, big data, psychological research, best practices for asking, and many other helpful resources are available. Setting these aside in favor of a *just show up and see what happens* attitude can become an excuse for laziness or a way to avoid difficult conversations possibly leaving donors confused.

The Strict Moves Management Approach

At the other extreme, a strict moves management[4] model entails

---

4 *Moves management* refers to planning a series of actions (AKA *moves*) designed to help a donor or other constituent move from the present reality to a desired future outcome (make a gift, attend an event, etc.). Examples of moves include a simple phone call and a complex overseas vision trip.

extensive planning and a somewhat formulaic approach to building relationships. If the donor says this, then do that. If the gift is a certain size, then do this.

While this approach offers value particularly to work with major and mid-level donors, it still falls short. Only following a highly scientific and data-driven model in relationships may result in a lack of sensitivity to plan changes or challenges in donors' lives, and it does not allow for nuanced conversations. As believers, we recognize the power of the Holy Spirit to lead and guide us, give us empathy, and give us courage to have conversations for which we may not feel equipped.

The Proverbs 16:9 Approach

The good news is there is an area in the middle of both of the previous approaches which combines their best values. Proverbs 16:9 says, "We can make our plans, but the Lord determines our steps" (NLT). Applying this passage to fund development ministry takes the mindset that strategically planning and managing moves in relationships still allows room for the Holy Spirit to work.

Taking the Proverbs 16:9 approach allows you to implement best practices, leverage research, and rely on data without sacrificing listening to God and how he may be leading or guiding in a donor conversation. Rather than either having tunnel vision or becoming overly focused on a hoped-for outcome, you can be flexible. Jesus did the same with Jairus' daughter in Mark 5:21–43. His disciples planned their day and how the girl would be healed. While the healing occurred, it happened according to Jesus' plan and not the disciples'.

Many years ago, Les, a major gifts officer with one of the world's largest Christian ministries, was on his way to visit a donor and dear friend of the ministry. Les prayed about his plans for the visit while he drove – plans which did not include a specific amount he should invite the donor to give. The Holy Spirit pressed him to ask for $50,000 for a people group in Africa. When he asked, the donor broke down in tears. Les thought, "I blew it, that must have been offensive. I just killed the relationship." However, the donor said $50,000 was the exact dollar amount that God laid on her heart during her morning devotions.

Moves Management within a Proverbs 16:9 Approach

The ministry that global mission organizations can offer to donors is tremendous and frequently overlooked. Many donors to Christian organizations report feeling like organization staff treat them like an ATM. However, when an organization's fund development staff believe that their work is about spiritual formation rather than transactions, donors become partners in as well as beneficiaries of ministry.

Paul says in Philippians 2:3, "Don't be selfish; don't try to impress others. Be humble, thinking of others as better than yourselves" (NLT). In missions organizations there can be a tendency to only apply this to work with marginalized and unreached people groups. It should also apply to donors and prayer partners that come alongside organizations in ministry! Interactions with donors should be a two-way street where each blesses the other.

FIVE PRIMARY PRINCIPLES FORM THE FOUNDATION of a healthy ministry-centered moves management strategy:

Listening

Each donor is a unique person made in the image of God with passions, dreams, fears, and needs. Active listening is one of the most powerful ways fund development professionals interact with donors. This may be a mid-level rep listening to prayer requests over the phone, a major gift officer learning why a donor is interested in a part of the world, or a survey of all active donors on communication preferences. In an increasingly distracted world, truly listening to donors and meeting them where they are

> # When an organization's fund development staff believe that their work is about spiritual formation rather than transactions, donors become partners in as well as beneficiaries of ministry.

(physically, emotionally, mentally, and spiritually) is a ministry organization's offer that donors may not experience in other areas of their life. Over time, active listening helps fund development staff anticipate each donor's questions, needs, and desires.

Praying

Many donors have few safe spaces to freely share prayer requests. Because an organization's fund development staff are usually not part of a donors' church community or family, donors may share private prayer needs with them. Sometimes they are the only ones who pray with and for donors about these particular needs! Fund development professionals occupy a unique position to minister to donors through prayer. This could be in person, over the phone, or simply through internal prayer bulletins that confidentially share donor prayer requests.

Inviting

I once talked with a friend who wanted to start a ministry. The friend's income allowed him to fully fund the ministry without raising additional funds. He said he wanted to avoid "begging" for money.

I responded, "I love the outline you just gave me for your ministry, and I want to be involved! If you specifically design the business model of the ministry so that you get the privilege of giving and no one else does, then you are robbing me of an amazing opportunity to be generous and make a major impact."

Organizations should invite prospective donors to give:

- *Without apology* – because God has called us to be a part of the invitation process. The donors' investment may be an answer to God's call on them.
- *Professionally* – because competence shows respect for their participation, and we are called to work "with all your heart, as working for the Lord" (Colossians 3:23, NIV).
- *As part of a team* – which includes prayer partners, donors, staff, etc., that works together as one body (2 Corinthians 12:12–27) to impact the mission.
- *Without guilt or manipulation* – because 2 Corinthians 9:7 says, "You must each decide in your heart how much to give. And don't give reluctantly or in response to pressure. 'For God loves a person who gives cheerfully'" (NLT).

Appreciating

Donor ministry does not end when a gift is received. From the initial acknowledgment and processing of the gift through implementation of the funds, donors should be treated with the highest degree of care. Gifts should be processed quickly and accurately. In fact, consider how your gifts processing team might recognize that they have a significant ministry opportunity to donors.

Donors should be thanked immediately, frequently and creatively. The prevailing wisdom in the nonprofit world has been that a donor should be thanked seven times for making a gift.

Whether an initiative went well or not, report openly and honestly about it.

Does this seem like overkill? Put yourself in the donors' shoes.[5] If you voluntarily contributed funds that could have been used on a dinner out, a trip to Europe or expanding your business, and all you received was a simple receipt to file with your tax papers, how would you feel? On the other end of the spectrum, what if you received a thank you call from a staff person a few days later, then a formal letter from the CEO a week after the gift, then a short e-mail from the beneficiary after the project went into effect, etc.? Now, on top of the joy of giving, you also see that the organization is grateful for receiving what you gave to them. This is key to establishing a true ministry to donors.

Reporting

You may be tempted to stop the moves management cycle at thanking the donor. However, one critical group of moves remains. Organizations should always report back on how the funds were stewarded and what happened as a result so that donors know the impact of their gifts. Whether an initiative went well or not, report openly and honestly about it.

---

5 One way to put yourself in your donors' shoes is to make a gift to your organization and track your donor experience. Or ask a friend to make a gift and have them tell you how they are treated. The online fundraising lab, NextAfter, made several fascinating discoveries in a research study they conducted called *The Mid-level Donor Crisis.*

Consider the fund development professional as a liaison between donors and the people groups the mission serves. In some cases, this might mean connecting the donor with end users or beneficiaries. For a major donor, this may mean a visit to the field. For a specific group or segment that gave to a particular type of work, it could be an update done by video or live conference call. Sending a regular newsletter or magazine to donors is another important move which connects the donor to the impact of their gift.

Conclusion

Analyzing your donor file will uncover a host of opportunities as your mission seeks donors to come alongside and participate with you in God's mission. Every donor in your file is a unique individual, church, or foundation that God leads. Some are a modern picture of the widow offering her mite (Luke 21:1–4) or David offering all of his gold and silver (1 Chronicles 29:1–9). God gives you the opportunity to minister to and with each of these funders and steward their engagement with global mission. May you humbly seek the Lord's help in ministry so that he receives all the glory!

CHRIS WINKLER is married to Christie, and they have three children: Judah, Jovelle and Josiah. They have served with Wycliffe Bible Translators for fifteen years, including five years in Nigeria. Besides ministering to donors, Chris enjoys reading history, hiking, and playing board games. The Winklers live in Orlando, Florida.

Chapter Reflections

- What is your personal view of fundraising? Do you see it as a necessary task to complete so that your *real work* can be done, or do you see it as a ministry to donors? How does your organization view fundraising?
- What do you know about how your organization's donor base is constructed? How could you pull from available data to build a simple strategy?
- Does your fundraising plan rely too much on moves management? Or do you avoid conversations which make you uncomfortable resulting in not inviting donors to participate in God's mission?
- What is one new or creative way your organization can thank or report to donors in response to their financial generosity?

Additional Resources

Burk, Penelope. Burk's Blog. https://www.burksblog.com/.
A blog that examines unique opportunities to minister to donors with research to back it up; provided by Penelope Burk of Cygnus Applied Research, Inc.

Nouwen, Henri J. M. *A Spirituality of Fundraising*. Upper Room Books, 2011. A small and powerful book perfect for all fund development professionals working for missions organizations.

Veritus Group. "Passionate Giving Blog™". https://veritusgroup.com/passionate-giving-blog/. A blog full of useful information about how to minister to donors.

CHAPTER 11

Creating Environments that Empower Relationships

By Steve Kaloper

I RECENTLY EMCEED A UNIQUE EVENT for a ministry we serve on the central coast of California. We do events all over the country for them, but for this one, we gathered in a beautiful coastal college town in an area with a lot of wineries to create an environment in which the ministry, Lifewater International, could engage with donors. We called the event "Wine into Water." Not surprisingly, the event was held at a winery.

Lifewater International is an organization of Christians committed to ending the global water and sanitation crisis. Their vision is to "see thousands equipped, millions served, and a movement of transformed people serving together to end the global water and sanitation crisis." We hosted the event at the winery not only to make the connection to Jesus' miracle in Cana of turning the water into wine, but also to create a memorable setting in which donors could learn more about the cause, see and hear about the impact gifts were already having, and feel safe

Originally published in a slightly different form in *The Journey into DoingGoodBetter*, Steve Kaloper (2015), chapter seven. Reprinted by permission of the author.

enough to consider partnering at a deeper level.

More than one hundred people attended the event where we heard about the ministry in a refrigerated tavern surrounded by barrels of wine. Talk about ambiance! We had an evening together in this historic winery next to the beach to showcase the cause and give them an opportunity to invest in it. Following the event, the daughter of the founder of the organization told me that the event was the best she had seen in forty years, and that her father would have been proud. The bottom line was that we deepened relationships with well over one hundred donors and raised nearly $120,000 in the process.

And it all happened because we intentionally created an environment that empowered relationships. I believe that environments are really where relationships happen – where donors can connect to the magic and power of your why. If you want to connect with today's major donors, you must create compelling environments in which they feel empowered to engage and can see, feel, or experience your organization's impact on the cause.

The Power of Environment

Environments can range in size from fifteen to twenty people gathered around pizza at a lunch-and-learn to larger weekend events for major donors. One of the most memorable environments I've ever had the privilege to be part of was a unique example of the power of the right setting to stir generosity with donors.

A number of years ago, I led a vision trip to Southeast Asia with Ravi Zacharias with about thirty people. The first few days were about getting the feel of the place and getting comfortable with one another, but after several days people started going deeper into conversations over meals. We started in Singapore for a couple of days, then went on to Thailand, Bangkok and other cities. We did a few traditional tourist activities, such as an elephant ride, but we also stopped at an orphanage in Chiang Mai, Thailand.

The home was run by a young woman in her mid-twenties. She was a survivor of the sex trade who had worked in the red-light district from the time she was thirteen years old. When she was sixteen, she became a Christian but was still trapped in that industry. I couldn't even imagine how hard it must have been to believe that what you were doing was wrong and yet still be compelled to participate. She finally escaped. Yet as she saw kids on the street, she realized that they were going to have the same fate unless someone intervened.

So she got a little bit of money, rented a little studio apartment, and started bringing in kids from the street. Now, several years later, she had a home she had mortgaged which is where we visited her and the orphans. Our hearts broke as we heard how she worked with the kids she picked up off the streets, gave them food and a place to sleep, and helped educate and mentor them so they wouldn't have the life she had endured. Her cause was front-and-center. She was clearly passionate about it, and we all could see she was getting results.

As we were preparing to leave, I asked her, "What is the burden that weighs the heaviest on you every day?" She answered, "the debt of this small home." She told me how much she owed – $413,000! As we boarded the bus to leave, everyone was pretty silent, just soaking it all in. Because Ravi is such a generous guy who recognizes God is an abundant God, he gave me the freedom to share what I had heard from the young woman about the mortgage on her house. After sharing the need, I simply said, "If anyone wants to help relieve some of the debt from this woman's shoulders, here's a piece of paper. Let's just pass it around." I didn't tell anybody the amount that she still owed. I merely said, "We're on the honor system. I'm not going to follow up with you. Don't put your names on the paper, just write down what you might be willing and able to give. It is what it is. I'm not even going to think otherwise if you just hand it to the person next to you. No one will."

We passed the paper around the bus. No one wrote their names

The right environment can make all the difference.

on the card, just the numbers of what they wanted to pledge. When it got back to me, my wife and I wrote down our pledge, and I totaled it up. The total amount of donations pledged just blew me away – $413,000! Within sixty days of coming back from the trip, all the money came in and the woman's debt was paid. She now had the freedom to focus on her cause without that burden on her back.

We all saw her passion, her mission was clear, and everyone had confidence in her ministry because it was endorsed by Ravi, myself, and others. I've seen many amazing things like that happen again and again to produce unexpected results for God's glory. The gifts pledged on that bus in Thailand were the result of the experience we had. The right environment can make all the difference.

Types of Environments

Environments can be sorted into a few major categories, but the names can change to fit your organization's vernacular. I find it helpful to talk about them with these basic labels:

- Small Gatherings
- Briefings
- Summits
- Larger Events

SMALL GATHERINGS might include events such as a vision lunch, a conference call, or one that we employ a lot these days – the lunch-and-learn. A lunch-and-learn is about sharing who you are and what you do, because most of the attendees probably don't know anything about the organization. For example, there is a great organization called Lifeline Children's Services that we've worked with to host lunch-and-learns. Most of the people who attended were on their lunch break and didn't know anything about the organization, but they cared about sustainable life and water solutions.

People used to have dessert gatherings in their homes, but the times have changed. Those kinds of events tend not to work as well as they did in the past. Today, a lunch-and-learn can happen just about anywhere. Lunch-and-learns are intentionally non-threatening, safe places where people can first learn more about your cause and get acquainted with your organization. A lunch-and-learn might start with a statement like this: "We want to share with you the landscape of prostitution in America," or, "We want to share with you what's happening in Birmingham on this issue." That's it. That's a lunch-and-learn.

For example, one time I was presenting with the Well House in Birmingham in a lunch-and-learn environment. As we wrapped up, I said, "Some of you might have been thinking about people that would have been great to have here today. Some of you might even have offices or teams where you run a small business. We'd love to order in some pizza and come in to share with the people in your office." That invitation led to a lunch-and-learn a couple months later in someone's office. They actually had someone bring in pizza and drinks as we shared the vision with twenty people.

BRIEFINGS are more elaborate and structured gatherings in which you are introducing your organization – who you are, what you do, and why – or an issue on which you are the experts in the room. There's no need for an ask because the event is for current donors and their friends. There is more detail as to the financial health of the organization and transparency about those aspects, often with visuals such as a pie chart. The environment strategy

A briefing is a great place for a donor to transition into a champion.

for a briefing is all about getting a donor to realize he or she is in a safe environment. When people feel as if they're in a safe environment, they can start to see themselves as a champion, and that takes time.

Whereas a lunch-and-learn is designed to fit within a lunch break, a briefing is usually an hour and a half to two and a half hours in length. In some cases, a briefing can be tailored for major or mega donors. The amount of preparing, planning, and people involved in a briefing depends on the organization. Part of the strategy is about working through donors to go deeper into their networks and communities of friends. Lunch-and-learns are a great place to start, but a briefing allows you to go deeper.

The briefing is designed for simplicity of presentation. But it's also designed for there to be openness for God to work in hearts as people connect their passion with yours. A superb briefing unites the elements of environment and setting with engaging story-telling to invite people into an experience. It's about more than articulating your mission clearly; it's about immersing people in your story, and making it come alive for them through compelling visuals and storytelling that balances details with a vision that engages at an emotional level. The best events share an organization's story with the listener in mind while blending the right mix of clarity and passion.

A briefing is a great place for a donor to transition into a champion. After the event we want everyone to invite their friends to the next one. So be sure you do set a date and time for the next briefing as you plan the initial briefing. By the time the first one is over, some major and mega donors may have people in mind that they want to invite to the next one.

Our most current briefing strategy focuses on moving people to become experts in the topic of the briefing. For example, our briefings for the ministry Faith Comes by Hearing focus on the great commission. We talk primarily about what God's doing to bring the Bible to the world and secondarily about how Faith Comes by Hearing is right in the middle of that movement by recording word-for-word dramatized audio of the Bible. So, the briefing is not about coming to learn about Faith Comes by Hearing, it's about coming to hear about the great commission. When we do these events, something subtle but powerful takes place. With fifteen to twenty-five people in the room, we create an environment that's intimate and relational enough that high-capacity donors are willing to come without fear of being cornered or badgered to give.

But what about the ask? With the Faith Comes by Hearing briefings, we tell attendees that this isn't a fundraiser. There are no pledge cards. If they care about the great commission, we invite them to invest strategically to shape a legacy that impacts eternity by funding a dramatized audio edition of an entire Bible, a chapter, or their favorite family verse. We've raised hundreds of thousands of dollars through events like this. We get emails from people afterwards saying they want to fund two entire languages now that they know the need.

SUMMITS are partnerships with other organizations around a cause that you share. The spotlight is placed on the cause and not any one organization. Organizations can say who they are and what they do, but not actively promote themselves. The end result is that donors connect with organizations who share their passion for a cause, and a door opens to go deeper into the relationship.

Take, for example, the topic of human trafficking in Atlanta. Rather than hosting an event that is all about your own organization, a summit approach would mean organizing a panel discussion or inviting a group of organizations to share with a larger

Donors connect with organizations who share their passion for a cause.

pool of donors about what is being done on a broader scale about the horrific practice of human trafficking. People gather at summits because they care about a cause, and in the process end up learning about five or six organizations. The strategy for a summit involves crafting an appropriate program and presenting it well, in addition to getting the right mix of organizations in front of the right audience to create a win-win environment where donors can find the best conduit to a cause they care about.

LARGER EVENTS might include mid-week dinners, galas, and weekend experiences, such as a founder's weekend or president's weekend, at which fifty to one hundred couples gather to engage with leadership and uncover the heart of the organization in a setting designed to facilitate the growth of the donor as much as to help the organization.

The donor cultivation process is the secret sauce to any such program. When we began to work with the Christian Medical and Dental Association (CMDA), we completely restructured their evening event. Their program previously featured fifteen minutes of praise and worship music, followed by an emcee introducing the speaker. The speaker would then talk about whatever he or she wanted to talk about. Then the emcee would make everyone aware of the pledge cards. The problem was that, although many people were willing to donate, the program really didn't tell them enough about the organization itself.

To reinvent their event, we chose to emphasize the three prongs of their strategy to introduce who they are as an organization. First, they serve a community of believers in the medical profession who seek to live out their faith in their medical practice. The second part was about local and global missions; they have a mobile medical unit for local missions, and they do medical trips through global missions. The third part was the mentoring that these medical professionals do for medical students on college campuses. The three-pronged approach outlines the crescendo of living the Christian life as a medical professional.

Their event still involved music and an emcee, but we added a dinner. Before the dinner got started, someone from CMDA spent five minutes explaining the mission of the ministry. He encouraged attendees to get to know one another during dinner. We had placed a CMDA host at each table who shared why he or she was involved and what they do. This table discussion really made the impact of the organization personal in a way a speaker on a stage never could do. After dinner the emcee brought onstage five medical students who had gone on medical mission trips to Peru over the summer. They all shared their incredible experiences, with one even tearfully adding, "I'm so proud to be a medical student because I get to be a part of this great community, and I can serve people with all of you."

The next piece of the program was a twenty-minute interview with a member of CMDA who runs the mobile medical unit in the area. He told about how many people they serve, the nuts and bolts of it, and why he's involved in running that program. He helped the audience to see why he, a doctor, gives up his Saturdays to run the unit. The tip of the arrow, as we had coached him to emphasize, was that he is a member of the Christian Medical and Dental Association of America. Because he was a member, he was inspired, empowered, and encouraged to do something about a terrible issue: human sex trafficking.

After that interview, we took all of seven minutes to reconnect the mission to the vision and close the event. There's a methodology to all of this. The common thread of every program for every organization is strategy, simplicity of the mission, the story of why we're in the room, and the experience. You have to bring people into the experience in order to have a life-changing impact on people's lives because of the organization, whether it be through personal testimonies, videos, or something else. Mission, story, experience, vision – and then the ask.

The ask requires a set-up at the beginning of the event. As the emcee for this event, I laid out the whole schedule of the program at the beginning: "Here is our journey for tonight. We're going to be very clear at the beginning about our ministry's mission. We're going to share the story of why we're here tonight and why we do what we do. We're going to have a panel of students talk about the impact of medical mission trips, and then we're going to hear an interview with a guest speaker. At the end we're going to share briefly where we want to be in the next twelve to thirty-six months, because later tonight we hope that our journey has resonated with you, and that we've earned your desire to partner with us, engage us, or support us financially." I mentioned the ask at the beginning because I wanted everyone in the room to know what was coming. It builds trust with attendees when you lay out a clear plan for the event and then stick to it.

Each of these types of environment brings its own unique challenges and benefits. And, of course, there are tactics specific to each of them that really make them shine as part of a comprehensive plan for engaging donors. I cover all of them in detail, including tactics, programming, and subtle nuances as part of our DSG Intensives.[1] But one additional example may help you see how all of them can work together.

How Environments Work Together

There is a ministry we've worked with for six years that does work in Middle East regions such as Iran. Back when I first met

---

1 For more information visit Development Services Group, https://developmentservicesgroup.com/.

them, Iran was in the news every day, and they were raising about $900,000 annually with fewer than a thousand donors. Their mission is to strengthen and expand the church in the Iran region and beyond. I helped them develop a strategy to capitalize on the interest in that region of the world. We started with lunch-and-learns called "Inside Iran." We went to community leaders and churches to let them know we wanted to help the Christian community understand what was happening inside Iran.

Over the course of a year, we hosted those events in ten cities and encountered more than three thousand people, most of whom couldn't even find Iran on the map! Some of them had heard of the Ayatollah, but didn't know that the Biblical characters of Ruth, Daniel, and the Persians had anything to do with the history of the Iranian people.

The first thirty minutes were just about the history of Iran. The second part was about what God was doing in Iran, how there was a hunger for a relationship with the Lord, and how in the last ten years the number of Christians there had multiplied from 100,000 to over 1,000,000. The third part was about this ministry and the work they were currently doing in the middle of God's movement in Iran: smuggling in Bibles, training new Christians through a program in Turkey, on-going discipleship, and church planting.

We hosted these lunch-and-learns for two years and then started to weave in other events like vision luncheons for donors. The ministry leader began to get invited to speak at summits for foundations that were trying to figure out what was going on in Iran. As more summit organizers heard, he began to get invited to be part of panel discussions as an expert on ministry in Iran. We added founder's weekends later, where we had one hundred people attend major donor meetings. In one such weekend, we raised several million dollars. We followed a similar pattern for two years: host a presidents' weekend with one hundred people, challenge them to become a champion by hosting a briefing in which we would condense that weekend down to three hours.

In five years, we grew their donor base from less than one

thousand to over four thousand. Their annual funding grew from $900,000 to over $6.5 million! And it all started with simple lunch-and-learns, which we strategically called "Inside Iran" so it would be relevant both to the audience and the organization's reason for existing – the why.

STEVE KALOPER is the founder and CEO of Development Services Group which offers fundraising strategies for nonprofits. He has over twenty years of experience in marketing and developing strategic relationships in the private, public, and nonprofit sector. In 2015 he authored the book, *The Journey into DoingGoodBetter*. He and his wife, Shannon, have four children and reside in Atlanta, Georgia.

Chapter Reflections

- What type of environments would work best for your organization or cause at this point in time: lunch-and-learns, briefings, a summit, or something larger?
- How might you adapt these environments to fit your unique organization and target audience?
- Do you have the necessary skill sets and experience on your team to create environments that unite story-telling with mission and empower deep relationships with donors?

Bibliography and Additional Resources

Kaloper, Steve. *The Journey into DoingGoodBetter*. 2015.

CHAPTER 12

Let's Get Personal

By Keith Sparzak

THE MEDIAN PRICE OF A HOME in Los Angeles, California is more than $700,000. The median home value in Wichita Falls, Texas is around $100,442. Why? Remember the realtor's mantra? "Location! Location! Location!" That is the ultimate determiner of a home's value.

My wife and I owned a beautiful turn of the century Victorian home in Grand Rapids, Michigan. First-time visitors often responded with "Ooohs!" and "Aaaahs!" when they entered that glorious space. And on the occasions, we hosted high net worth people with their own very expensive homes, even they expressed how attractive ours was.

We bought our home in 2000 for only $128,000. We sold it twelve years later, after numerous improvements, for $153,000. It could have cost over $750,000 to rebuild at that time! Although our home was beautifully crafted, in great condition, and hard to affordably replace, the market price was painfully low. The location, while decent overall, was in some ways less than desirable. This reduced its value relative to its quality and character. Again, what mattered was "Location! Location! Location!"

In the philanthropy world there is another mantra: "Relation! Relation! Relation!" It is a critical factor that many Christian donors and foundations use to determine the ministries for which they will give and at what frequency. For some, relationships are nearly the *only* factor they consider.

It's Challenging but Not Impossible

I spent nine years as a program officer at a well-known Christian foundation. Over those years, I met with hundreds of ministry leaders, development directors, and representatives across a spectrum of organizations who were attempting to acquire funding for their ministries. Their fundraising skills varied from excellent to ... not the best.

Fundraising is difficult for most ministry leaders and reps. It takes a solid combination of communication techniques, winsome personality traits, professional acumen, ability to respond well to spontaneous questions, and people skills to do it with consistent excellence. While it still may not be *comfortable*, what is not hard for most, even introverts, is personally connecting with others. Basic techniques, which rely on sincere curiosity and not manipulation, can help form a relational bridge between a person raising funds and a potential donor.

As a foundation program officer, I determined which projects would be recommended to our board. This role carried significant influence. I could have easily assumed an elitist posture toward ministry representatives. In fact, from time to time, I observed that attitude in other foundation program officers. It made me nauseous. Pride should make anyone nauseous! I didn't want to be "that guy."

When I served on the global outreach team of a large church, a senior colleague and mentor intentionally and repetitiously taught our team about humility. He instructed us to always assume a sincere posture of humility and pursue relationships with anyone, regardless of their status. This became one of my major goals. I purposefully went out of my way to genuinely connect with any person I met. I continued this in all my subsequent roles.

> **Always assume a sincere posture of humility and pursue relationships with anyone, regardless of their status.**

It has made a tremendous difference over the years.

My efforts did not go unnoticed, especially when I led conversations with personal questions. Asking about a person's family, spouse, children, or grandchildren evoked responses such as "Thank you for asking! Nobody from your country has ever asked me about my family before!"

Think about that for a moment. At best, that's an embarrassing indictment. At worst, it's sinful. These are members of our Christian family and co-laborers in the kingdom. They deserve more than a sterile transaction. They deserve a *relationship*. Engaging ministry leaders that way helped me develop dozens, if not hundreds, of meaningful global friendships. Intentionally putting extra time and effort into first getting to know the person with whom you want to financially partner results in a significant return on investment.

You might think, "Wait a minute. You are talking from a former donor's perspective. How does this apply to the ministry leader or representative raising money?" My answer: "Turn the table." Leaders and ministry representatives who look for resources must also be highly intentional in getting to know a potential donor. Demonstrating genuine interest in knowing a donor personally, rather than simply "getting down to business" and presenting your resource needs, should be a primary goal.

Unfortunately, what I said about potential donors who did not take time to get to know ministry leaders or reps is overwhelmingly true of the ministry leaders I interacted with, too. Woefully few

Connecting well with people in spite of cultural and personal idiosyncrasies takes research, intuition, and experience.

ventured to ask me about personal matters related my family, my faith journey, my interests, and so on.

Granted, sometimes this can be excused by the power difference many feel between donors and recipients. Fund-seekers can perceive that it may not be appropriate to, or they may not have the freedom to, ask a potential donor personal questions or to be too casual. While understandable, this is an unfortunate misconception. Careful engagement with and sincere interest in a potential donor or donor representative is typically welcomed and enhances the interaction. It helps put people at ease and gives donors the sense that they are not human ATMs.

Cultural dynamics are also at play. In certain cultures, it really is inappropriate to ask personal questions too early in a relationship. But with a little help from someone familiar with the culture, you may find ways to overcome this challenge. Connecting well with people in spite of cultural and personal idiosyncrasies takes research, intuition, and experience. It is critical to intentionally invest in learning about interpersonal and cultural dynamics.

Connect Authentically

Building authentic relationships is so important for trust, rapport, and *chemistry*. What fund-seekers need to work toward, especially in the early stages, is an affinity through shared vision, values, experiences, and ministry focus. A meeting with a potential donor is not a failure if you have not been invited to the next family wedding. It is a *success* if you sense that some level of mutual respect and positive chemistry was attained. Getting to this point takes work. These four key contributors will get you on your way to establishing authentic relationships: time, humor, humility, and appropriate preparations.

Time

Relationships cannot be imposed on someone who may not be enthusiastic about the idea. Genuine relationships take time. Going too hard, too fast or too deep – *especially too soon* – may not yield the results you desire. Recognize that each relationship develops differently, and most develop slowly. As the relationship develops, so does trust.

My wife and I frequently go camping, and I usually build fires for these occasions. Even after building hundreds of fires, I still want to hurry the burn and move too quickly from spark to inferno. As soon as I see a flame, I often throw on larger pieces of wood and smother the fire. I was a boy scout for only two weeks which may explain this pathology!

Sometimes ministry leaders and fund-seekers operate like this. They expect too much too soon. First time, longer term, and multiple granting arrangements almost always are rooted in time-tested, trust relationships. Also keep in mind that relationships with funders still must be coupled with adequate ministry performance. But assuming that a ministry is accomplishing its mission well, trust becomes the main catalyst for ongoing grant activity with that ministry. Trust moves a donor to invest resources to a ministry's kingdom endeavors.

Time is a key factor in establishing trust. You can't go from a first date to a wedding in one meeting! Even if a flame is burning, fund-seekers need to go slow lest they smother the fire by throwing on the logs too soon. One time a ministry leader chastised me during one of our initial meetings because he was dismayed that I required he complete a grant application for his project. He said this was evidence that I did not trust that his ministry would use the funds as they'd committed to verbally.

I found out later he'd lodged the same accusations at others. But these procedures come from an acknowledgment of the Bible's teaching on the Fall and the sin nature. And experiences from foundations like ours supported this – not all ministry leaders used funds in the way for which they committed they would be used. Time invested in building an accountable relationship is necessary for a successful outcome. Needless to say, this ministry leader's exhortation to just trust him without investing time in our process resulted in no application and no grant.

Humor

Humor can be a powerful way to connect. While cultural dynamics can make humor more difficult, many aspects of comic relief work across cultures. If it's not a strong skill for you, you may not want to try it when meeting with donors. But this is a mistake and a missed opportunity. Laughter bonds. Find ways to use it.

Years ago, during my days at the foundation, I was in the *courting mode* with a well-known missions agency. I had established a positive and growing relationship with their development director. When he found out that I would be attending a mission forum that he and his CEO planned to attend, he arranged a meeting during the event between his CEO and me.

This development director insisted on making a quick intro of his CEO and then leaving the two of us on our own. I began my usual round of questions about family, ministry background, and so on. Early in the conversation I noticed a respectably large spider slowly making its way up the CEO's arm toward his neck. I interrupted him and said, "Pardon me, friend, but you might like to know that there is a spider crawling up your arm." Without a twitch or batted eye, he reached across with his other arm, carefully removed the spider, popped it into his mouth, chewed two to three times, swallowed, and continued talking without missing a beat.

At this point, he could have been pitching an income generation project selling sandbags to nomads in the Sahara Desert, and I would have said, "SOLD!" Well … maybe not. But he definitely won me over through his off-the-wall action and established a stronger relational bond with me through his humor. Now I do not recommend carrying a box of edible arachnids to an interview with a potential donor, but do try to use humor to connect.

Humility

I wrote earlier about a former senior colleague and mentor that encouraged humility and the profound and positive impact that had on me as I continued my ministry career. I urge fund-seekers to adopt this same posture. Potential donors usually will not know your ministry and its context like you do, but you do not need to dismiss them. However, sometimes the depth of their knowledge may surprise you!

I remember one meeting in Central Europe with a leader who didn't treat me this way. He acted as though I needed to read a *Missions For Dummies* publication! He was so convinced of my ignorance that he didn't want to share the name of his ministry location because he was certain I would mispronounce it. His near disdain for the lack of knowledge he thought I had of his culture and context was palpable. This obviously did nothing for our relationship. If he had instead related to me with humility, he may have learned that my ancestors, in fact, came from his region! Listen to donors even as you expect them to listen to you. You might gain something beneficial for your ministry.

In another meeting in Asia, I met with a leader with a wall of pictures of him shaking hands with *important* people. He took me through the photos pointing at each one-by-one and then summarized saying, "I am a very important man, as you can see," or a dynamically equivalent phrase. After a long *talk-a-thon* about his relevance in the kingdom, the meeting concluded. I think I

Part of preparing is knowing how to address questions a potential donor may ask about your ministry, your metrics, your impact, and so on.

refused to have a picture taken of me shaking his hand before I left. The relationship didn't go any further and neither did a grant. Always embrace true humility; it's a good companion.

Appropriate Preparation

Preparedness is a double-edged sword. Being underprepared makes an initial encounter awkward because there is a lack of content to meaningfully engage ... and who likes feeling awkward? Conversely, overprepared pressures the presenter to get through all the material to the detriment of deeper-level dialogue, which can then short-circuit relational development. So, it's critical to strike the *right* balance. Part of preparing is knowing how to address questions a potential donor may ask about your ministry, your metrics, your impact, and so on.

I once met with a ministry leader introduced to me by a colleague without an existing relationship with this leader. The brother we connected with was probably a good man doing good kingdom work. However, he barely said anything. During the long gaps in our conversation, we simply sat and stared at each other or looked around the room without saying anything. In an hour-turned-eternity we left with barely a clue of what he actually did or what he hoped we could do in response to our encounter. It was the most awkward meeting EVER!

On the other extreme I once met with a ministry rep that had thirty PowerPoint slides, four double-sided, ten-page handouts, and six supporting video testimonials. My memory could be exaggerated, but you get the point. Some overprepare for good reasons, while others do so to simply try to impress with copious amounts of content. Avoiding both ends of the spectrum is a good practice and contributes to confidence, trust, and authentic relationships.

It's Not That Complicated

Have you ever seen on a Facebook profile under the *Family and Relationships* section the phrase "It's complicated?" Personal relationships can be complex and thorny. But developing and retaining ministry funding relationships are typically straightforward. Really. Just be intentional, present your ministry well, and perhaps most importantly, practice habits that will grow lasting relationships.

Good relationships require trust and authenticity. You can't fake your way to fund-seeking success through manipulation. The mission and vision of your effective ministry can become an invitation to others to partner with you. But keep in mind the mantra of the philanthropy world: "Relation! Relation! Relation!" It will yield a significant return on investment that will help your ministry to grow and flourish.

KEITH SPARZAK has served as international director of Community Bible Study since 2016. He oversees the development and implementation of strategies, mission critical activities and assists his team in Colorado Springs to support regional and national directors, as well as volunteers, in the one hundred twenty countries where CBS has a presence. He previously served for nine years with a Christian foundation as a program officer, and twenty years in a variety of pastoral positions: global outreach, as well as associate and lead roles.

Chapter Reflections

- How would measure your relational intelligence on a scale of one to ten (with ten being very strong)? How would your friends and peers rate you? Ask some of them for an honest assessment.
- Reflect on a time when someone related to you poorly in a collaborative ministry relationship. Identify the elements that caused you to consider it as a poor experience. Do the same while recalling a successful one.
- Develop a list of achievable action steps that will help you to sharpen your cultural/relational intelligence skills for the sake of becoming a more genuinely relational leader. Execute the steps.
- Try role-playing with an associate implementing the learning you gleaned from the above action steps – within the context of approaching an imagined potential donor.

Bibliography and Additional Resources

Buchanan, Phil. *Giving Done Right: Effective Philanthropy and Making Every Dollar Count*. PublicAffairs, 2019. This book covers a broad swath of subjects related to philanthropy. His observations on the role of relationship in partnerships are very insightful.

Cultural Intelligence Center. "About Cultural Intelligence." https://culturalq.com/about-cultural-intelligence/. Livermore's website has a wide spectrum of cultural intelligence assessment tools and resources to help people become more cultural aware, astute, and confident in their ability to relate well with people from a variety of backgrounds.

Livermore, David. *Leading with Cultural Intelligence: The Real Secret to Success*. AMACOM, 2015. Written by a Global Leadership Summit speaker, this book has much to say about relating cross-culturally. Livermore works globally with both Christian and non-Christian entities.

Nouwen, Henri J.M. *A Spirituality of Fundraising*. Upper Room Books, 2011. This is an excellent short work which speaks to the heart attitudes of those doing fundraising, emphasizing that it is an activity for which we should have no hesitation conducting.

Petersen, Jonathan. "Relationships are Purpose Partners: An Interview with Dharius Daniels." February 6, 2020. https://www.biblegateway.com/blog/2020/02/relationships-are-purpose-partners-an-interview-with-dharius-daniels/. This brief article is an interview with Dharius Daniels, author of *Relational Intelligence: The People Skills You Need for the Life of Purpose You Want*, and speaks to the critical nature and role of, as Daniels calls it, purpose partners. While this article and Daniel's book do not speak specifically to the role of relationships in fundraising and philanthropy, the principles can be easily transferred into that context.

CHAPTER 13

Developing Partnerships with Major Donors and Foundations

By Barbara Bowman

ONE OF THE MOST SIGNIFICANT ENDEAVORS of a successful development program is major gift cultivation. The primary role of a major gift officer is to build trusting, long-lasting relationships with high-capacity donors. These high-capacity donors include both individual major donors and foundations. Either way, your work is to find those who have a love and passion for giving, a commitment to making a difference, and an alignment with your organization's mission. Because your organization is only one of hundreds if not thousands of global mission organizations, the long-term challenge is to develop partnerships with donors and foundations that feel ownership for your organization's mission. To see this happen, you must commit to building enduring relationships.

Building Relationships with Major Donors

Why Are Major Donor Relationships Important?

Each donor's motivation is complex and connected to psychological or spiritual factors. While intellect is not absent from their philanthropic decisions, their spirit and aspirations tend to lead

As much as 80% of an organization's income will come from 20% of their mid to high capacity donors which means these relationships are not only important, they are also strategic.

their decision-making process. Many are motivated to make a personal difference in the kingdom of God through financial resource stewardship. However, it is relationships that sustain a donor's motivation to give over the long term.

Relationships take time. They usually begin with an introduction and then repeated encounters with casual conversation which leads to in-depth information exchanges. Over time, this nurtures confidence and trust. Eventually, the relationship becomes familiar, informal, intimate, and enduring.

Donor relationships typically follow a similar trajectory. Moving through the relational stages requires time, perseverance, and consistent connection. It can take an entire year to secure an introductory meeting with a busy donor, so it is critical that the major gift officer role is not a revolving door. Keep in mind that high capacity donors are often courted by as many as ten to twelve organizations at any given time.

As Claire Axelrad says, "Around every nonprofit organization in this country, there is a group of men and women, ranging in size from a half dozen to a few hundred, who hold in their humble hands the make or break power for the institution itself."

In fact, as much as eighty percent of an organization's income will come from twenty percent of their mid to high capacity donors which means these relationships are not only important, they are also strategic. If you have this mindset, then donor activities become part of fostering intentional trust relationships with partners. With careful cultivation, expect their growing passion for your organization's mission to lead to increasing gifts and eventually your organization being included in their estate plans.

Major Donor Game Plan author Patrick Mclaughlin provides a useful framework in his book for cultivating relationships between development representatives and donors: *communicate, educate, host, inform, invite, involve, love, network, notice, personalize, share, sympathize,* and *understand*; then once a gift is received from a donor, he suggests the following: *thank, honor, recruit, ask,* and *upgrade.*[1] Moving through these steps requires forethought and intention. This is true for even the most talented, seasoned fundraising professional.

How Do You Prepare for Intentional Follow-Up?

Keeping your donors engaged for the long-term requires a relational follow-up strategy. For instance, a birthday card can be followed up by a call to hear more about what they did that day. Mailing the annual report can be followed up with a call to see if a donor noticed how the project they supported has met major milestones. Follow-up is more important than any other activity because it keeps the relationship moving forward. Every donor activity needs a follow-up plan including events. Here are a few ways to plan for follow-up after a donor event:

- Have attendees fill out their name, address, email, and phone number when they arrive at an event.
- Have a notecard that lists several ways an attendee can get involved. Pre-print it with the donor's name on it and the organization's address, so they can mail it in on a later date.

---

1 Patrick G. McLaughlin, *Major Donor Game Plan* (Grand Rapids, MI: The Timothy Group, Inc., 2006), 87–90.

- Equip staff who attend the event to capture all pertinent information they learn from interacting with donors and enter it into a central database where it can be added to the donor's record.
- Send thank-you notes and then follow-up with a voice call to discuss next steps of engagement.
- After the event, invite prospective donors to another meet-up, a tour of your main office, or a conversation with an executive or staff member serving abroad.

Ultimately you want to forge allegiance to your organization. The more relationships and accessibility to those relationships a donor has in your organization, the more he or she will feel like part of the team or family. As your major gift officers connect donors and guide them through next steps, they need to take the passions, interests, motivations, and rhythms of each donor into account. This requires listening. In the early stages of the relationships, your major gift officers should plan to only speak twenty percent of the time. Equip them with a set of thoughtful questions. Consider these examples:

- What difference do you personally want to make in the world?
- If you could change one injustice in the world, what would it be?
- How does your faith shape your community, nation, or the world?
- What organizations do you love to invest in and why?
- What is the history of your involvement with our organization?
- Is there anything you would like me to sensitively share with our organization's CEO?
- With what organizations do you (or your spouse) volunteer and in what ways?
- What program do you feel highly invested in at our organization?

Keep the donor's passion and interest at the forefront.

- What is your heart's cry for your family or faith community?
- How can I be praying for you?
- What questions can I seek an answer for you?

If you listen before speaking, keep the donor's passion and interest at the forefront, and have honest answers to their questions, the relationship will develop naturally. But not every donor wants the same level of relationship. This must be discerned and respected. On one extreme you will have donors that desire complete anonymity and request no contact. Take that request seriously. On the other end, you will have donors desiring a sense of community and belonging. These donors need follow-up that connects them with opportunities to participate in events, vision trips, volunteer opportunities, or perhaps even the chance to serve on your board.

Donor cultivation also involves follow-up that leads to specific calls to action which enable donors to expand their impact. Donors want to know how they can help, what specific needs exist, and how their contribution can make a difference. Many genuinely want to be *asked* for a particular amount. Without any solicitation, a donor may believe there are no current needs or that you are too timid to ask them to participate financially.

Long-Term Relationships Yield Long-Term Engagement

Most organizations hope a donor volunteers, prays and contributes for the long haul. Relationships are at the heart of this long-term investment. Because major gift officers typically serve two years, they need to see their role as a facilitator, aligning the donor to the organization, rather than focusing on deepening their own personal friendships with donors. It is a bridge-building role with the gift officer taking the lead in helping a donor make a variety of organizational relationships.

A donor cannot remain dependent on a gift officer. If a gift officer leaves, a donor's affinity to the organization and giving level should not change. When a gift officer focuses on facilitating relationships, it can look like arranging meals with other organizational staff with a gift officer purposefully being absent. It could also be arranging a vision trip for a donor with an executive to deepen their relationship with staff at your main office and on the field.

Major gift officers also play an important discipleship ministry role which further contributes to facilitating long-term engagement. God implants in each of his followers a desire for a generous, selflessness, and sacrificial life, but some people get distracted and controlled by the pursuit of amassing money. It is impossible to serve money and God. Gift officers can encourage those they connect with regularly to be live generously and put their complete trust in God (1 Timothy 6:17–19).

Income should be the resulting *fruit* of intentional relationship-building. It will come as you are faithful in the small intentional activities. You will know if you are on solid footing if you labor looks like this:

- You focus on the personal goals of the donor and what he or she can accomplish through their investment in your ministry.
- You appropriately steward your donor's time and availability.
- You seek out donor input and advice about your organization even if you disagree with what they share.
- You show patience and empathy with a donor's traits, canceled appointments, and strong opinions.
- You allow a donor to determine their level of involvement with your organization.

- You solicit gifts in a straightforward and honest way.

With a sincere effort to do the above, progress will be made year after year. Relationships will deepen, the organization will become more accessible, your donors will grow in their faith, and charitable income for your organization will increase.

Building Relationships with Foundations

Where Do You Begin in a Foundation Relationship?

Building healthy, long-lasting relationships with foundation staff is nuanced and different from individual major donors. Often foundation staff only focus on relationships with nonprofits with active grants or ones they intend to fund in the future. With potentially hundreds of inquiries, letters of intent, or grant applications coming their way, they need to be selective about who they spend their time with and how. For this reason, foundation relationships need a strategic approach that maximizes time and effort. Begin with research. See if mission alignment exists between a foundation's funding priority and your organization. Prioritize relationships with foundations and their staff where your mission aligns well with their goals and objectives.

Take note of other organizations that have received funding. Call their grants department or head of development and ask questions about what factors contributed to other organizations successfully receiving grants. Leave the conversation with names, titles, and contact information of staff that make decisions or can help you in significant ways. If a foundation does not list grant awards on their website, ask a grantee the size of their grant or the range of the customary award. Lastly, ask a current grantee if they would be able to facilitate an introduction to a foundation program director or administrator or allow you to use their name in the prospecting process.

Once you determine that your nonprofit is a good match for

Prioritize relationships with foundations and their staff where your mission aligns well with their goals and objectives.

a foundation, it is time to create a prospecting strategy. It can take several years of courting a foundation before you receive an invitation to submit a grant. Your primary objective at this early stage, then, is to get the attention and interest of a foundation's staff or trustees. Take opportunities to tell them about your excellent work, your measured impact, and your future goals and objectives.

One simple way to do this is to mail your annual report to them with a cover letter attached. You could also draft an exclusive *outcomes* report for foundations and send one once or twice a year. More personal ways to connect could be to invite a foundation representative to your annual donor weekend, host foundation staff for a tour of your main office, or if they will be traveling to a region where you have active projects, ask them to visit one of your projects. This "come and see" approach is useful in helping a foundation representative catch a vision and get excited about your organization's impact.

How Do You Grow and Maintain a Foundation Relationship?

If the door is open, move towards building a relationship before submitting a first grant. A voice call is adequate, but an in-person meeting is better. If possible, get an appointment to personally meet with the foundation staff before submitting a grant application. Request no more than an hour of their time and stick to it unless they invite you to stay longer. Consider bringing your CEO with you and make sure he or she is well-versed on the foundation.

Before launching into the mission and impact of your organization, ask them about their history, current funding goals and objectives, advice, or encouragement they might be willing to share. After you have listened and learned, share succinctly about your organization's mission and strategic initiatives. Then ask them questions that will guide your process in the future. For example, you might ask if they fund capacity building, if they like restricted projects, or if they fund multi-year or shorter-range projects. If you have piqued their interest and they have researched your organization ahead of time, be prepared to answer a wide range of questions. After the visit, follow-up with a thank you note and additional information.

Once you receive the good news that you are a grantee, you are responsible for meeting grant requirements including reports and updates. However, the relationship also remains critical. Consider having the board chair or even a program director that will be impacted by the grant write a thank you note rather than just the executive director or development director. Invite the foundation to visit the project they are funding. If the project is not playing out as planned, be proactive, and reach out to the foundation. The staff wants the project to succeed so they can help provide solutions or link your team to other resources.

You will likely not always have an active grant, but you will still want to maintain the relationship. Request to be added to the foundation's e-newsletter or annual report list. Ask for an invitation to any conferences or forums which you could attend in the future. If you find any reports or other content related to their area of investment, consider mailing or sending a link to them with information. Add them to your regular organizational communication. And lastly, think about making an annual visit to let them know what your organization is currently doing.

Foundation staff can change often. If you know a change is coming – a program director is leaving or a representative is changing positions – ask for an introduction to the new staff person. If that is not possible, reach out to the new staff person once he or she is in place to make an introduction. Stay in contact to make it easy for foundation staff to stay connected with your organization.

Conclusion

Relationships between donors and nonprofit organizations need to be stewarded well. Not all relationships will be long-term. Some are only for a season. But trust that God always has reasons to bring people passionate about his kingdom and living out the gospel together. Stewardship begins with prayer and a servant's attitude. God can do so much more than the best-laid plan or strategy. Count on donors and foundations investing in God's work to have high integrity and a humble spirit. When approached in the same way by development staff, a relationship can be bridged easily and quickly. Trust and transparency are the hallmarks of a respectful and robust bond, not based on wealth or money, but on the same passion for serving God and humanity. Add time and healthy communication, and your seeds will reap a bountiful harvest.

BARBARA BOWMAN holds a bachelor of science degree in guidance and counseling with an emphasis in career management from Colorado Mesa University. She has more than thirty years of experience in nonprofit management and corporate career management including nine years as the vice president of advancement for a US$46 million global faith-based nonprofit. She and her husband live in Boise, Idaho. They have two adult children.

Chapter Reflections

- What are three to four steps that you can immediately take to improve your donor relations efforts?
- Why do your high-capacity donors give to your organization? Have you asked them this question or are you making assumptions?
- As you build relationships with donor couples, what strategies can be uniquely effective with each person?
- What three or four leaders in your organization would your donors love to engage with based on their interests?

Bibliography and Additional Resources

Axelrad, Claire. "Clarification: Philanthropy, Not Fundraising." https://clairification.com/.

Johnson, Larry C. *The Eight Principles of Sustainable Fundraising: Transforming Fundraising Anxiety into the Opportunity of a Lifetime*. Aloha Publishing, 2011.

MacDonald, Gordon. *Generosity: Moving Toward a Life that is Truly Life*. GenerousChurch, 2010.

McLaughlin, Patrick G. *Major Donor Game Plan*. The Timothy Group, Inc., 2006.

Perry, Richard, and Jeff Schreifels. *It's Not Just About the Money: Second Edition: How to Build Authentic Donor Relationships*, 2nd ed. Veritus Group, 2020.

CHAPTER 14

Building Effective Relationships with Foundations

By David Broussard

IN THE SUMMER OF 2018, I made a presentation at a grant conference to about fifty full-time grant professionals about the marriage of two of my passions – grant work and prospect research/management. My goal was to provide insights about how to respond to the never-ending call from leadership to find new funding, particularly, in the form of *grants*.

The presentation described each stage of research and engagement. Everything was going well until I got to *cultivating the relationship*. Immediately, four or five hands shot up, and I heard murmurs and discussion around the tables. We spent the rest of the time swapping stories about the challenges we faced when trying to build relationships with foundations. "How do we build strong and effective relationships with foundations?" is likely the single most asked question among grant professionals.

A Different Kind of Relationship

Establishing relationships with foundations is not intuitive. Typical major donor relationships with an organization begin with a list of prospects generated through a form of acquisition. After new donors give a first gift, organizations work hard to under-

Foundations are not faceless giving machines.

stand these donors, what they care about, and how deeply they want (and can) be financially engaged in advancing the cause. Their first gifts indicate support of your organization's mission, but you don't know their charitable giving patterns or capacity. Even prospect research will only take you so far, so the best you can do is estimate giving capacity. You only learn more through deepening your relationship with each donor individually.

The world of foundations is the complete opposite. The foundation's assets and how much they give away is public information. Foundations even calculate their giving on a rolling five-year average to maintain their tax-exempt status (by United States law, foundations must give away five percent of this average every year). You can find out exactly who receives the money and how much is given to each organization. Their board members names (and sometimes their addresses) are available publicly. Sometimes the foundation even notes the purpose of the funding in great detail on their tax return (990-PF) or provides valuable information on their work and passions on their website.

All of this data and *inside* knowledge – and the sheer number of foundations that match particular criteria – create a dangerous environment where development professionals can be tempted to skip the needed work of relationship building and move forward with a mass appeal – creating a mail merged proposal to send to dozens, even hundreds, of foundations. This *spray and pray* approach rarely yields desired results.

Organizations that learn to avoid this pitfall discover that the key to working with foundations is building strong relationships. Yet how do you engage foundation decision makers when you have very little *relational* data? While there is no *proven* formula, there are best practices your organization should consider as you try to advance in the world of foundation funding.

Step One: Reframe Your Mindset

Every foundation's primary goal is to make good investments in projects and organizations that align with their mission. As stewards of financial resources, they work to find organizations and projects that achieve their goals and objectives. Remembering that the foundation's decision makers are stewards of God's resources in God's mission – just like you –instills a *partnership mindset* in your interactions.

Keeping this mindset throughout all your interactions can facilitate conversations with the foundation and an understanding of how they work. Your goal is not to "get the grant" but to discern whether or not this will be a good partnership. Is there alignment, affinity and interest? Foundations are not faceless giving machines. Storming the gates short-circuits relationships. Go slow, be positive, and give grace. Realize that if you seek understanding and dialogue in appropriate and genuine ways, developing foundation relationships becomes more productive for both parties.

Step Two: Do Your Research

If your goal is to establish a strong relationship with a new foundation, your first contact must be well-researched in order to begin and keep the relationship moving forward. The less you know about a foundation, the more likely you will make a serious mistake in your initial approach. Investing in research will give you the best possible chance to begin a real dialogue. A skilled prospect researcher can do this for you. But if you do not have anyone doing that for you, below are focus areas you can use to research foundations on your own.

STUDY A FOUNDATION'S STRUCTURE AND PROCEDURES. Foundations are made up of people who steward God's resources through structures, by-laws, policies, and procedures. Each has their own process for awarding grants. Study those processes. If a foundation says don't do *X* or do *Y*, they mean it. Take their words at face value.

BE AWARE OF THE TIMING OF YOUR INTERACTION. If a foundation has a June 15 deadline for *Letters of Inquiry* submissions, do not try to meet or call them on June 18. Their staff will likely be knee-deep in submission evaluations. It's bad timing. Put yourself in the shoes of the board and staff and consider their workload. Then plan accordingly.

LEARN ABOUT THE ROLES AND RESPONSIBILITY OF A FOUNDATION'S LEADERSHIP TEAM. Who are the board members? What are their titles? Are they compensated? Do they have paid staff, program officers, or administrators? Just like policy and procedure, staffing and leadership reveals how a foundation works. Knowing this will help you decide who to reach out to and what to say. For example, your approach to a small family foundation with no staff and unpaid board members who are all family members is different than it would be with a foundation that has unrelated board members and a paid grants administrator.

FIND OUT THE NUMBER OF GRANTEES AND MOST COMMON GRANT AMOUNTS. Knowing the number of grants a foundation gives and their amounts helps organizations understand a foundation's grant-making rhythm. A foundation that makes ten grants of $5,000 each year is different from a foundation that makes one hundred grants of $30,000 per year. The time and effort foundations need to process requests will also be very different in those two scenarios as would their way of operating. This helps you keep appropriately sized grants in mind to discuss if a conversation develops.

DISCOVER THE CONNECTIONS BETWEEN YOUR ORGANIZATION AND THE FOUNDATION. Many organizations don't do enough research on the front end to unearth their connections with foundations. Having your board review a list of foundations and their board members to see if there are any existing relationships is a critical step, but it is not the end of the process. Find and subscribe to relationship mapping tools such as *ProspectVisual.* If your budget is tight, go on LinkedIn and Facebook to find personal or professional connections between your organization's staff, board, and donors and the foundation. Target specific cities and regions by pulling a list of constituents (past and current donors, board members, volunteers) and then seeing if any of those people know the foundation's board members. Also look for overlapping professional associations or groups.

Step Three: Do a Realistic Assessment of Your Organization

Foundations expect greater transparency than your organization may be used to with other donors. They may ask you to submit information about your operating budgets, shortfall explanations, audited financials, board/staff ethnic and gender diversity policies, outcomes, evaluation, and internal strategic plans with any proposal you submit. They will also expect that you clearly know who you are as an organization. Your organization needs to prepare all of this information in advance so you can go as deep as a foundation wants to go with you. Waiting until they ask is too late.

When you know the criteria that are important to foundations, you can implement robust organizational assessments to ensure you meet their requirements. As a part of your assessment, evaluate who on your team holds each piece of this information and their readiness to prepare it for you. If your organization isn't ready to do this, then developing a relationship with a foundation will end in disappointment. So, before you even call a foundation, make sure you and your team are prepared with what you know you'll need and be ready to gather more data if it is needed.

When you do your internal assessment, do not fall into the trap of believing that because your organization received funds from foundations in the past, that it is grant ready now. Foundations each have their own giving standards and not all issue grants. Grants require outcome reporting and have well-defined application processes. If a foundation is less formal in their giving, assign them to a major gift officer who can work with the family. If a foundation instead uses a sophisticated grant making approach, cultivate your relationship through grantseeking efforts adapted to the robust processes of institutional funders.

Finally, out of all the criteria in an internal assessment, reputation is an organization's biggest asset or downfall. Foundations that have a strong mission match with your organization may already know about you. Foundations know many more organizations than they support through proactive research, curiosity, rumors (yes, they exist), peer discussions, and even reports from the field. Foundations usually understand the nonprofit space better than organizations think. Therefore, when assessing your organization, take into account any recent scandals, controversies, or issues that could have damaged your organization's reputation.

I spoke with an organization recently that consistently presented themselves as if they were the only ones working in their field, when they weren't. They told me about several well-known foundations that had supported them in the past, but they didn't know why that support stopped. They never followed up with the program officers or executive directors. Was their reputation damaged by overinflating their work or their outcomes? Were they trying to hide something? It wouldn't surprise me to learn that their claims damaged their reputation, and then word got out in the grant making community.

Step Four: Make a Plan and Execute It

After finding foundations with mission and granting aligned with your organization's mission and activities, a good next step is to create an *engagement plan*. This is a one to two-page document that compiles all your research on a foundation and includes action steps to engage them. Here are suggestions for ways you can begin to build an engagement plan:

GATHER BASIC INFORMATION ON THE FOUNDATION. Name, contact details/person, website address, area(s) of focus, the history of the foundation, past interactions/history with your organization, assets, giving history, highest grant recipients (their favorites), and whether or not they accept unsolicited requests (if yes, the process to submit those requests).

COLLECT ESSENTIAL INFORMATION ON STAFF. Names, titles, contact details (when appropriate), and connections your organization has to foundation board members and staff.

CREATE AN INITIAL APPROACH STRATEGY. This should outline who will make contact, in what way, and what information they will need in advance of reaching out.

An initial approach strategy depends entirely on what information is discovered during the research phase. If there is a relational connection, plan it out well. The goal is for a volunteer, board member, donor, or staff to have a good experience reaching out to a connection at a foundation. Your organization needs to fully support and guide that connection especially if a volunteer has offered to use their own connections and networks on your behalf. If a connection is best made by email, then your organization needs to draft an email and a series of responses for negative or positive answers from a foundation. If the initial contact will be made by phone, have a comprehensive script.

If your organization does not have a relational connection, you have two options: wait for a connection to happen through networking – attending events where foundations may be or mobilizing your major supporters to form a fundraising committee to enlarge your networks – or make a cold call. Many times, a cold call is the only option. You may feel apprehensive about making a cold call, so here are several tips for doing it successfully:

REMEMBER YOUR ATTITUDE AND MINDSET. Your initial objective is not to get money or make a grant request. You are seeking to listen, understand, and learn about the foundation in your mutual pursuit to discern the potential of partnership.

DON'T TRY TO GO TOO FAR TOO FAST. A foundation staff person answering a cold call doesn't know what they are *walking into*. Honor them by clearly presenting yourself and why you're calling so they can respond with appropriate guidance and direction.

DISCOVER YOUR AREAS OF MISSION OVERLAP. Briefly share about your organization's work and then ask the foundation staff person questions to see if there are opportunities to pursue common interests together.

The best result for a cold call is a meeting with a program officer or executive director to discuss each other's work and missions to see if there is a path forward. Should that not be possible, often sending information about your organization to the foundation by mail and following up on that correspondence is the only option. In your follow-up communication, remember that your organization needs to offer the foundation a strong value proposition: a new perspective on the work they're already funding; potential collaboration with their current grantees; a way to accomplish their mission in greater and more cost-efficient ways; etc.

Craft your communication well. Make it highly customized and brief with a follow up step that focuses on learning from the foundation and their reactions to and thoughts on your organization's work. If you do speak to someone, send a thank you card addressed to that person to thank them for their time. Include a card in case they need anything related to your work. Be persistent but respectful. If there is strong synergy, seek to partner with some of their current grantees and make contact once a year to wish them well and share a quick testimony or snippet of your work.

Conclusion

Establishing foundation relationships takes time and persistence. Foundation grant cycles and decision-making processes are much longer than individual donors. Organizations need to plan eighteen to twenty-four months of regular and highly customized relational overtures before being able to submit a proposal (which may be declined on the first try). Patience, persistence, and investments of personnel and finances are all required for organizations seeking to partner with foundations and build lasting relationships with them. But the work is worth it. A successful process will secure more long-term funding for your cause and mature your organization's ability to serve.

DAVID BROUSSARD is a certified grant professional (GPC) and has worked in nonprofit development since 1997. He is fluent in French and is the founder and president of Impact France (www.impactfrance.org) which has facilitated over $8.5 million in giving to national French ministries. He has a bachelor's degree in French from Dickinson College. He and his family live near Atlanta, Georgia.

Chapter Reflections

- What examples of successful and unsuccessful relationships has your organization had with foundations in the past? What differentiated the successful from the unsuccessful ones?
- What element in foundation relationship building strategies is the most difficult for your organization to execute and why? What are ways that you can overcome this?
- What expectations have you had when thinking about grants and foundations? Did this chapter challenge any of those? If so, how?

Bibliography and Additional Resources

Foundation Source. "What Is a Private Foundation?" https://foundationsource.com/learn-about-foundations/what-is-a-private-foundation/. Go to this site to learn more about private foundations.

Excellence in Giving. "Case Studies." https://www.excellenceingiving.com/case-studies. These case studies offer helpful narratives about Christian foundations and grant makers.

Professionals in Christian Philanthropy. "About Professionals in Christian Philanthropy." https://pcpcommunity.com/about/. This is a website for Christian grant makers.

GEO. "What we care about." https://www.geofunders.org/what-we-care-about. This is a website for secular grant makers.

Appendix

Aly Sterling Philanthropy. "How to Write a Development Director Job Description: 4 Key Tips." Last updated September 30, 2017, https://alysterling.com/development-director-job-description/. While this is not a faith-based source, it has good guidelines.

Andringa, Robert. "What Is the Board's Role in Fundraising?" ECFA, https://www.ecfa.org/Content/What-Is-the-Boards-Role-in-Fundraising-NP. A good basic article on this subject.

Axelrad, Claire. "Clarification: Philanthropy, Not Fundraising." https://clairification.com/.

Buchanan, Phil. *Giving Done Right: Effective Philanthropy and Making Every Dollar Count*. PublicAffairs, 2019. This book covers a broad swath of subjects related to philanthropy. His observations on the role of relationship in partnerships are very insightful.

Burk, Penelope. Burk's Blog. https://www.burksblog.com/. A blog that examines unique opportunities to minister to donors with research to back it up; provided by Penelope Burk of Cygnus Applied Research, Inc.

Candid Learning. https://learning.candid.org/. This site offers free and paid grant courses and sessions.

Center for Theory of Change. https://www.theoryofchange.org/. Go to this site to learn more about theories of change and logic models.

Collins, Jim. *Good to Great and the Social Sectors: Why Business Thinking is Not the Answer*. HarperCollins, 2005. This book will help you understand how a nonprofit runs and where fundraising fits into its economic engine.

Crutchfield, Leslie. *Forces for Good: The Six Practices of High-Impact Nonprofits*. John Wiley & Sons, 2009. Review the case studies to learn more about successful nonprofits.

Cultural Intelligence Center. "About Cultural Intelligence." https://culturalq.com/about-cultural-intelligence/. Livermore's website has a wide spectrum of cultural intelligence assessment tools and resources to help people become more cultural aware, astute, and confident in their ability to relate well with people from a variety of backgrounds.

Doolittle, Cameron. *Joy Giving: Practical Wisdom from the First Christians and the Global Church*. Rophe House, 2018.

Evelyn and Walter Haas, Jr. Fund. "UnderDeveloped." Last updated January 14, 2013. https://www.haasjr.org/resources/underdeveloped.

Excellence in Giving. "Case Studies." https://www.excellenceingiving.com/case-studies. These case studies offer helpful narratives about Christian foundations and grant makers.

Foley, Eric. *Coach Your Champions: The Transformational Giving Approach to Major Donor Fundraising*. .W Publishing, 2010. This book offers specific guidance on building a major gifts program.

Foundation Source. "What Is a Private Foundation?" https://foundationsource.com/learn-about-foundations/what-is-a-private-foundation/. Go to this site to learn more about private foundations.

GEO. "What we care about." https://www.geofunders.org/what-we-care-about. This is a website for secular grant makers.

Gibson, Cynthia M. "Beyond Fundraising: What Does It Mean to Build a Culture of Philanthropy?" Evelyn and Walter Haas, Jr. Fund, https://www.haasjr.org/sites/default/files/resources/Haas_CultureofPhilanthropy_F1_0.pdf.

Grant Professionals Association. https://grantprofessionals.org.

Gravelle, Gilles. *The Age of Global Giving: A Practical Guide for Donors and Funding Recipients of Our Time.*

Hoag, Gary G., R. Scott Rodi, and Wesley K. Willmer. *The Choice: The Christ-Centered Pursuit of Kingdom Outcomes*. ECFAPress, 2014.

Johnson, Larry C. *The Eight Principles of Sustainable Fundraising: Transforming Fundraising Anxiety into the Opportunity of a Lifetime.* Aloha Publishing, 2011.

Kaloper, Steve. *The Journey into DoingGoodBetter.* 2015.

Kanter, Beth, Anne Wallestad, Linda Wood, Katrina VanHuss, Andrea McManus, Jann Schultz, Cheryl Contee, Wendy Watson-Hallowell, Pamela Barden, and Russell Pomeranz. *Fundraising Matters: Building a Culture of Philanthropy.* Blackbaud Institute, 2017. https://institute.blackbaud.com/asset/npexperts-2017-fundraising-matters-building-a-culture-of-philanthropy/.

Lencioni, Patrick M. *The Ideal Team Player: How to Recognize and Cultivate the Three Essential Virtues.* Jossey-Bass, 2016.

Livermore, David. *Leading with Cultural Intelligence: The Real Secret to Success.* AMACOM, 2015. Written by a Global Leadership Summit speaker, this book has much to say about relating cross-culturally. Livermore works globally with both Christian and non-Christian entities.

MacDonald, Gordon. *Generosity: Moving Toward a Life that is Truly Life.* GenerousChurch, 2010.

McLaughlin, Patrick G. *Major Donor Game Plan.* The Timothy Group, Inc., 2006.

Miller, Mark. *The Secret of Teams: What Great Teams Know and Do.* Berrett-Koehler Publishers, 2011.

Mission Increase. https://www.mif.org/. This organization has helpful resources for learning more about fundraising and training courses that may be useful for new fundraising hires.

Nouwen, Henri J. M. *A Spirituality of Fundraising.* Upper Room Books, 2011. A small and powerful book perfect for all fund development professionals working for missions organizations. It speaks to the heart attitudes of those doing fundraising, emphasizing that it is an activity for which we should have no hesitation conducting.

Panas, Jerold. *Asking: A 59-Minute Guide to Everything Board Members, Volunteers, and Staff Must Know to Secure the Gift.* Emerson & Church Publishers, 2013.

——. *The Fundraising Habits of Supremely Successful Boards: A 59-Minute Guide to Assuring Your Organization's Future*. Emerson & Church Publishers, 2012.

——. *Mega Gifts: Who Gives Them, Who Gets Them*. Emerson & Church Publishers, 2005.

Perry, Richard, and Jeff Schreifels. *It's Not Just About the Money: Second Edition: How to Build Authentic Donor Relationships*, 2nd ed. Veritus Group, 2020.

Petersen, Jonathan. "Relationships are Purpose Partners: An Interview with Dharius Daniels." February 6, 2020. https://www.biblegateway. com/blog/2020/02/relationships-are-purpose-partners-an-interview-with-dharius-daniels/. This brief article is an interview with Dharius Daniels, author of *Relational Intelligence: The People Skills You Need for the Life of Purpose You Want*, and speaks to the critical nature and role of, as Daniels calls it, purpose partners. While this article and Daniel's book do not speak specifically to the role of relationships in fundraising and philanthropy, the principles can be easily transferred into that context.

Professionals in Christian Philanthropy. "About Professionals in Christian Philanthropy." https://pcpcommunity.com/about/. This is a website for Christian grant makers.

Reis, Jeremy. "25 Interview Questions to Hire Your Development Director." Nonprofit Donor, https://nonprofitdonor.com/25-interview-questions-to-hire-your-development-director/. This article offers a solid list of interview questions.

Rodin, R. Scott and Gary G. Hoag. *The Sower: Redefining the Ministry of Raising Kingdom Resources*. ECFAPress, 2010.

Rodin, R. Scott. *The Third Conversion: a Novelette*. Colbert, WA: Kingdom Life, 2015.

——. "How Much Is Enough?" Produced by ECFA. *Excellence in Ministry*, May 1, 2019. MP3 Audio. https://excellenceinministry.podbean. com/e/how-much-is-enough-scott-rodin/.

Social Transformation Project. "Tools & Resources." http://stproject.org/resources/.

The Alford Group. "Culture of Philanthropy: Assessing the Culture in Your Organization." https://alford.com/wp-content/uploads/2014/09/Culture-of-Philanthropy-Assessment-Grid-Updated.pdf.

The Chronicle of Philanthropy. https://www.philanthropy.com/. Purchase a subscription to this periodical to stay up on nonprofit fundraising trends and gain access to their webinars and toolboxes.

The Grantsmanship Center. https://tgci.com/. This site offers comprehensive, paid training.

Thomas, Steve. *Donoricity: Raise More Money for Your Nonprofit with Strategies Your Donors Crave.* Lioncrest Publishing, 2018. This book explains how to craft fundraising messages.

Veritus Group. "Passionate Giving Blog™". https://veritusgroup.com/passionate-giving-blog/. This blog, full of useful information about how to minister to donors, offers insights in fundraising and major gifts fundraising in particular.

Made in United States
Troutdale, OR
12/23/2024

27210917R00110